GAUGUIN

Gauguin

by René Huyghe

CROWN TRADE PAPERBACKS · NEW YORK

Title page: SELF-PORTRAIT WITH PALETTE, 1893–1894
Oil on canvas, 36¼″ x 28¾″ (92 x 73 cm)
Private collection
Courtesy Acquavella Galleries, New York

Series published under the direction of:
MADELEINE LEDIVELEC-GLOECKNER

Illustrations and layout:
MARIE-HÉLÈNE AGÜEROS

Translation:
HELEN C. SLONIM

Copyright © 1988 by Bonfini Press Corporation, Naefels, Switzerland

Published by Crown Trade Paperbacks, 201 East 50th Street, New York, New York 10022.
Member of the Crown Publishing Group.

Random House, Inc. New York, Toronto, London, Sydney, Auckland

CROWN TRADE PAPERBACKS and colophon are trademarks of Crown Publishers, Inc.
Originally published in hardcover by Crown Publishers, Inc., in 1988.

Printed in Italy - Poligrafiche Bolis S.P.A., Bergamo

Library of Congress Cataloging-in-Publication Data

Huyghe, René.
Gauguin
(Crown art library)
Translation of: Gauguin.
1. Gauguin, Paul, 1848–1903. 2. Painters—France—
Biography. 3. Painting, French. 4. Painting, Modern—
19th-century—France. I. Title. II Series.
ND553.G27 H813 1988   759.4   88-7082

ISBN 0-517-88416-X

10 9 8 7 6 5 4 3 2 1

First Paperback Edition

THE MARKET GARDENS AT VAUGIRARD, 1879. Oil on canvas, 26″ × 39½″ (66 × 100.3 cm)
Smith College Museum of Art, Northampton, Massachusetts

During the nineteenth century man first became conscious of his evolution throughout history, but the amplitude and brutality of such changes were only fully perceived during our time and art is essentially the intensified reflection of this perception. At the end of the nineteenth century, Impressionism closed one artistic era and opened up another one. While it carried realism to the apex of its achievement, it also signed its death warrant because it offered a vision of nature that was too subtle, too "artistic" for contemporary viewers to recognize it as their own. Thus modern painting was born: From that time on, it became progressively less important to copy and respect every appearance of nature, the imitation of which had seemed for centuries to be art's supreme goal. Unwittingly, the Impressionists had a share in this revolution, but they only started it rolling. A new pictorial vision, unparalleled in several centuries, was achieved by

Paul Gauguin and Camille Pissarro, 1883
Self-portraits. Pencil
Musée du Louvre, Paris. Cabinet des Dessins

the generation following the Impressionists around 1885 — a generation that started to drift away from, even react against Impressionism, in spite of the admiration it felt. Paul Gauguin was the most radically daring and perhaps the most creative among these newcomers. In June 1899, he could write from Tahiti to Maurice Denis, one of the theoreticians of the new movement, that "The first part of my program has yielded its fruit; today you can dare anything and, furthermore, nobody is surprised." This generation of 1885 was responsible for the upheaval of traditional ideas. Its artists ceased to believe that they should follow nature. They considered instead that their creativity lay in the gap between the usual aspect of things and the vision which they offered. Gauguin alone, however, served this revolution with such radical demands and complete lucidity of aims and means. In this sense he deserved more than anyone else to be called the creator of modern painting.

GAUGUIN THE PRECURSOR

In a famous sentence, Gauguin emphasized what separated him from the Impressionists: "They sought around with the eye and not in the mysterious depth of the mind." Thus the new group proposed a new approach around 1885. These artists were aware of their demands and contributions; they offered to art a truth which no longer existed in the outer world, but only in the artist's mind and sensation. Not one of them, however, dared to go at it with as much resolution and lucidity as Gauguin.

Georges Seurat reconciled optical truth and abstract calculations of forms, where nature fell into mathematical harmonies. Paul Cézanne still respected and even sought the proper sensations, but he could not separate them from an intellectual approach, which defined simple and carefully arranged masses. Both artists completed and heightened sensations to the point of beauty, but at no moment did their mind substitute itself for, or contradict a sensation. They dared not yet tear and throw aside the veil of appearances, they wanted only to make it transparent. Progressively, however, they gave rise to constructions of the mind behind that veil. Behind the perception of things, the concept took on a significance similar to that of a skeleton, hidden by flesh which it holds together. They intimated, without yet allowing it, the eviction of reality by the plastic form, which the Cubists and Abstractionists offered us some time later.

Vincent van Gogh, like a tempest from the north, was butting with all his strength, and with no calculation whatsoever, against a routed nature, stirring it like a sea raised and plowed by the wind, or like a forest taut and buckling under a cyclone. He molded it in such a way that the viewer, seeing it thus overturned, forgets nature and is aware only of the twisting blast. Reality yielded to expression and a new trend was born, which led to Fauvism and Expressionism.

Self-Portrait, ca 1892
Crayon, wash, and watercolor
7¼" × 11⅝" (18.5 × 29.5 cm)
Private Collection
Courtesy Robert Schmit Gallery, Paris

Gauguin upheld both these trends toward plastic form and expression that were emerging around 1885 and were to rule the development of modern art. He showed a definite audacity, hampered only by an atavistic need to spare reality, to leave it intact. He broke off from the objectivity to which painting had been compelled earlier and thereby broke deliberately with six centuries of Western tradition. Claiming the right to absolute subjectivity, he chose to depict some elements of nature only as the material necessary to imprint thought and sensation. He went even further: He killed two birds with one stone and found in this subjectivity the possible

Profile of Boy, 1886
Pen and ink drawing
Breton Sketchbook, No. 16 (100.23 verso)
6½″ × 4¼″ (16.5 × 10.8 cm)
The Armand Hammer Foundation, Los Angeles

fusion point between plastic form and expression that were to divide modern art and sometimes pull it in opposing directions. He suggested that both approaches lead to the powerful emotional impact and personality of line and color alone.

Gauguin was perhaps less carried away than others by genius, but he was all the more lucid and determined in his quest. "With a lot of pride, I finally got a lot of energy and I have willed to will," he wrote in a text intended for his favorite daughter Aline. His intelligent and stubborn strength took him further still, opening new roads that Odilon Redon was the only other artist of the time to explore as well. Further than the plastic form, further than the expression of known feelings, he sensed the soul's submerged, still untouched recesses, the power of which could retemper our aging and refined civilization. Redon said that "Everything is done by a quiet submission to that which the unconscious brings." Gauguin was to be fascinated also by the unutterable and the problem of finding its language. He was to try and discover how to suggest the unspoken for lack of being able to explain it, how all that which speaks to the senses — line, color, picture — also speaks to the soul, for which it bears a mysterious meaning beyond reason and logic. Like Redon, he anticipated the further development of modern art, and half opened the door to Surrealism. And the name of the Dada movement may have been suggested by a yearning to "our childhood's rocking horse" (*le dada de notre enfance*, "dada" being French baby talk for horse) which Gauguin mentioned, [1] rather than a meaningless word chosen at random as it is proposed in the Larousse dictionary.

Gauguin was the first to emphasize the existence and significance of artistic schools that undertook the systematic exploration of the unconscious, but he seems to have

(1) *Noa Noa.* Paris: La Plume, 1900.

SLEEPING BOY (ÉMILE GAUGUIN), 1881.   Oil on canvas, 21¼″ × 28¾″ (54 × 73 cm)
Ordrupgaardsamlingen, Charlottenlund-Copenhagen. Collection Wilhelm Hansen

MADAME METTE GAUGUIN, 1884
Oil on canvas
25⅝″ × 21⁵⁄₁₆″ (65 × 54 cm)
Nasjonalgalleriet, Oslo

STUDY OF A NUDE (SUZANNE SEWING), 1880
Oil on canvas
45¼″ × 31½″ (115 × 80 cm)
Ny Carlsberg Glyptotek, Copenhagen

THE GARDEN IN WINTER, RUE CARCEL, 1883. Oil on canvas, 46″ × 35½″ (117 × 90 cm)
Private collection. Courtesy Acquavella Galleries, New York

prepared even further developments. While he was fully aware of three-dimensional and emotional resources to which modern art both dedicated and limited itself, and while he opened all the possible aesthetic explorations, he never reduced art to such an experimentation. He felt that painting can, indeed must, express fully the artist's inner life, that it can be limited neither to sensations, nor to ideas, nor to emotions, but that it commits the soul and its mysterious complexity. More than any other painter, Gauguin used art to serve this soul, which stretched beyond the limits of consciousness. He satisfied the aesthetic pleasure, but he also showed the need to go beyond this pleasure as well as the means to do so. He never forgot the rule of poetry, which surpasses all others and demands that the artist avoid "sterile exercises" and fulfill his own humanity.

This is the result of Gauguin's struggle, for which our century is heavily indebted to him, but he did not bring this wealth to light without unceasing painful efforts, and his was a slow conquest. Unhurried and powerful, Gauguin was now and then seized by a creative fever, but he was upheld primarily by strength. He fulfilled himself only through obstinacy and patience.

Landscape at Pont-Aven, 1886
Pen and ink drawing
Breton Sketchbook, No. 16 (100.24 verso)
6½" × 4¼" (16.5 × 10.8 cm)
The Armand Hammer Foundation, Los Angeles

This bold and dogged energy was his pride and mainstay throughout his difficult and sometimes desperate life. He could write to his wife, who was a prodigy of spiritual incomprehension as far as he was concerned, "I am working under unfavorable conditions and one needs to be a Colossus to do what I do under such circumstances." Up to his death he waged a hard struggle to draw his personality and art from his life and from himself. Indeed, he wrote, "I have willed to will."

THE HARD
AND SLOW VOCATION

Nothing came easily to Gauguin, he had to ascertain everything through will and strength, including his vocation as a painter. His rivals in fame wanted and knew to be artists from the beginning, while Gauguin discovered himself only gradually. The sea was his first calling and he was an assistant pilot and then a sailor from 1865 to 1871. Then, looking for a job, he worked for eleven years for a stockbroker as a half-commission man. During that time he became very well-to-do and was even able to build up a collection of Impressionist paintings.

Little Breton Boy Carrying a Jug, 1886
Pencil and crayon
Breton Sketchbook, No. 16 (100.38 recto)
6½" × 4¼" (16.5 × 10.8 cm)
The Armand Hammer Foundation, Los Angeles

Little Breton Boy Carrying a Jug, 1886
Pencil and crayon
Breton Sketchbook, No. 16 (100.38 verso)
6½" × 4¼" (16.5 × 10.8 cm)
The Armand Hammer Foundation, Los Angeles

14

One day, however, the consuming monster of art entered his life. Because of the usual habit of romanticizing famous lives, this conversion has been regarded as a brutal crisis, a bolt from the blue, an impulsive act, or, as Somerset Maugham called it, "a spell" which tore him from his established job, his home, his family obligations, and threw him into a creative venture. Apparently, this was not the case. Gauguin was strong, a slow, silent nature, with many dreams, but he steadily strived to turn those dreams into reality. His whole life was nothing but a stubborn race toward mirages and recurrent disillusions, except in art. More space would be needed to analyze step by step the transmutation which changed a well-to-do and bourgeois stock-exchange broker into a pareo-clad uncompromising artist who took refuge on a distant island in the South Seas to lead the Maori's primitive existence. No breaking point, no leap, but a gradual and stubborn gliding.

In 1873 he married a Danish girl whom he had met in Paris, Mette Gaad, a straightforward, practical woman, who was narrow-minded and deeply conventional. They had five children in ten years. Painting crept in, however. He had learned to love art when he was very young, at the house of his guardian, Gustave Arosa, a collector. He met some artists, notably Camille Pissarro, who was often a guest at his home; he started collecting; he painted in his spare time and took part in the Salon of 1876; thus he was driven slowly toward the vocation which was to consume him eventually. In 1880, he rented a studio on the Rue Carcel and joined the Impressionist group. He took part in the fifth Impressionist exhibition, and again for three consecutive years. Critics, and J.-K. Huysmans in particular, showed interest

Seated Breton Girl, 1886
Charcoal and watercolor on laid paper
12″ × 16⅝″ (30.5 × 42.2 cm)
Musée des Arts océaniens
et africains, Paris
Gift of Lucien Vollard

Little Breton Boy
Pencil and crayon
Breton Sketchbook, No. 16 (100.4 recto)
6½″ × 4¼″ (16.5 × 10.8 cm)
The Armand Hammer Foundation, Los Angeles

in his work. In 1883 he reached the breaking point. Events followed swiftly: He quit the stockbrokerage firm. This decision, however, seems to have been less spontaneous than it has been alleged, because a financial depression was causing many employees to be discharged at the time. He decided to devote himself entirely to painting. Life became difficult. Mette was not prepared to put up with sacrifices that seemed pointless to her, and, when Gauguin arrived in Denmark with wife and children toward the end of 1884, his in-laws were not too pleased. It has often been said that the artist abandoned his family to listen to the call of art. There again, as in the matter of quitting his job, the truth is less simple: The correspondence between Mette and Gauguin, after they had separated, brings ample proof of the pressure that was made on Gauguin to force him to leave. He would not, otherwise, have felt the right to write such sentences as "Now that your sister managed to make me leave.... Your brother claimed that I was in the way.... I was struck a hard blow.... I am put out of my own house.... Do not worry, your lapses are forgiven.... In spite of the way you hurt me, which I will not forget...", and on April 3, 1887: "Today I feel no more resentment against you...."

What impresses one most in Gauguin's outset is the absence of a spontaneous and self-assured creative power. He does not seem to be stirred by an inner demon demanding that he express himself and forcing the artist to discover his own idiom at all costs. What comes across instead is the patient labor of a man who has a feeling that his work will achieve greatness, but who still does not understand the nature of his art or the way to achieve it. Gauguin wanted to be a great painter, he felt an undefined possibility in himself. He aspired to be an artist and forged

MARTINIQUE LANDSCAPE, 1887. Oil on canvas, 45⅝″ × 35¹⁄₁₆″ (116 × 89 cm)
National Gallery, Edinburgh. Collection Maitland

PICKING MANGOES, 1887
Oil on canvas, 24″ × 45⅝″ (61 × 116 cm)
Vincent van Gogh Foundation
Rijksmuseum Vincent van Gogh, Amsterdam

18

BY THE POND, 1887
Oil on canvas, 21¼″ × 25⅝″ (54 × 65 cm)
Vincent van Gogh Foundation
Rijksmuseum Vincent van Gogh, Amsterdam

THE ROMAN BURIAL GROUND AT ARLES, 1888. Oil on canvas, 36″ × 28⁹⁄₁₆″ (91.5 × 72.5 cm)
Musée d'Orsay, Paris

ahead like an explorer crosses arid lands to see the promised city disclose itself one day. But this art was not yet present, it did not pull at his heart and soul to demand expression.

Even when he returned from Arles, when he was definitely free from Impressionism and had begun to find his own style, Gauguin hesitated still. In a letter to Emile Bernard — which the latter dated from 1889 in Arles and which was obviously written in Le Pouldu, in Brittany, that same year[1] — Gauguin revealed his doubts: "In my inner self, I think I can glimpse something higher. How I groped this year! My God (I kept saying to myself), I may be wrong and they may be right. This is why I wrote to Schuff [Schuffenecker] to ask for your opinion so as to help guide me in the midst of my confusion." Glimpse, grope, guide me, confusion ... all these terms are quite indicative. In another letter from Le Pouldu — Bernard dated it from 1890 but crosschecking seems to place it in the fall of 1889 — he added: "I am in a frightfully sad depression, while doing some work which will take time to be completed. There is a certain pleasure in not progressing in what I had prepared before, but in *finding something more. I feel it but cannot express it yet.*[2] Under the circumstances my *groping* studies can only yield ignorant and clumsy results.... What I want is a corner of myself as yet unknown." Patiently laborious, he explored methodically his own deep and receptive sensitiveness.

Two Breton Women, 1889
Pencil and crayon
Breton Sketchbook, No. 16 (100.49 recto)
6½" × 4¼" (16.5 × 10.8 cm)
The Armand Hammer Foundation, Los Angeles

(1) One should be most cautious in taking into account the order, place, and date of the letters published by Emile Bernard. His memory constantly misled him, and his data should be checked before being used as a source. He dated a whole series of letters "Arles, 1889," while Gauguin left this town at the end of 1888.

(2) The italics are the author's.

BLUE TREES, 1888.   Oil on canvas, 36¼″ × 28¾″ (92 × 73 cm)
Ordrupgaardsamlingen, Charlottenlund-Copenhagen. Collection Wilhelm Hansen

ABOVE THE ABYSS, 1888.   Oil on canvas, 28¾″ × 23⅝″ (73 × 60 cm)
Musées des Arts décoratifs, Paris

Pastoral Scene, Martinique, 1888
Zincograph on yellow paper
8⅜″ × 10⅜″ (21.3 × 26.3 cm)
Bibliothèque d'Art
et d'Archéologie
Fondation Jacques Doucet, Paris

Such was Gauguin in 1875 and it may be interesting, having followed his career, to follow also the development of his art. He started by shaping his craft, and was influenced by the Impressionists, whose works he collected, and by Camille Pissarro in particular, of whom he saw quite a lot and whom he chose as a master. At first, his approach was quite passive, although he showed a stubbornness portending future growth. He accepted the program of the new school, the content of which agreed with the beliefs of the late nineteenth-century bourgeois society, in spite of sharp contradictions in matters of form: Art is imitation, a reproduction of reality. The quarrel was only about the difference in opinion as to the means, traditional or new. Gauguin chose the latter, but not in the extreme. His colors remained in the muted range which, from François Bonvin and Henri Fantin-Latour to Jean-Charles Cazin and Jules Bastien-Lepage, seemed to further the solemn realism of Jean-François Millet that Pissarro admired so much. His palette was close to that of some paintings by Armand Guillaumin, Pissarro's friend and protégé. Gauguin met Guillaumin before leaving for Denmark and he certainly felt some affinity with this man who, while painting, kept his job as a clerk.

Gauguin's painting restricted itself to gray and brown tones lit by a few patches of deep blue and bluish green, calling to mind a heavy humus which was to feed the seeds later deposited by will and an exacting intelligence, a humus rather than such live element as water or fire. Vincent van Gogh, it is true, molded a still heavier clay in his earlier works, but his feverish hand gave it impatient convulsions, which were not to be found in Gauguin's dormant matter. This long phase of pensive sadness brought inner revelations to both artists, which were never given to the Impressionists. It was this sadness — more than a preoccupation with costs, which was only an added factor — that took Gauguin, along with Charles Cottet, Nubiens, Dauchez, and Lucien-Simon, to the solitary and gloomy Brittany, a province of granite and resignedness, where he first went in 1886. The Impressionists felt much more at home in the spruce outdoor cafés in the outskirts of Paris and the lively boat races at Argenteuil. As a consequence, Gauguin was attracted only by some among the Impressionists. Because of the masters who had made him love painting when he had admired their works hanging on the walls of his guardian, Arosa[1] — Jean-François Millet, Gustave Courbet, Camille Corot — he preferred to such brilliant Impressionists as Claude Monet and Auguste Renoir, with whom he never got along and whose *Moulin de la Galette* (Musée d'Orsay, Paris) dated from 1876, the more solemn representatives of the movement: Camille Pissarro (at the Salon of 1880 Huysmans regarded Gauguin's works as a "diluted version of the still uncertain works of Pissarro"); Paul Cézanne, who influenced him deeply, to the point that he could reproach him later of having stolen his "little sensation." While Gauguin met Cézanne at Pontoise in 1881, where he had joined Pissarro, the works by Cézanne that he had seen at the first Impressionist exhibition were clearly-defined paintings with muted colors such

(1) G. Arosa got him the job with the stockbroker Bertin.

The Grasshoppers and the Ants
ca 1889
Zincograph
7⅞" × 10⁵⁄₁₆" (20 × 26.2 cm)
Bibliothèque nationale, Paris
Cabinet des Estampes
Archives ERL

Breton Landscape: The Willow, 1889
Oil on canvas
36¼″ × 28¾″ (92 × 73 cm)
Private Collection
Courtesy Robert Schmit Gallery, Paris

The Yellow Haystacks
(The Blond Harvest), 1889
Oil on canvas
28¹⁵⁄₁₆″ × 36⅜″ (73.5 × 92.50 cm)
Musée d'Orsay, Paris

27

L'Arlésienne: Madame Ginoux, 1888
Charcoal, black and red crayon heightened with
white chalk, 22⅛″ × 19⅜″ (56.1 × 49.2 cm)
The Fine Arts Museums of San Francisco
Achenbach Foundation for Graphic Arts
Collection Dr. T. Edward and Tullah Hanley

as the *House of the Hanged Man* (ca 1873, Musée d'Orsay, Paris). Finally, Edgar Degas, who liked his work, did not turn him away from this sad and solid style. What a contrast between *The Seine at the Pont d'Iéna*, with its thick winter painted by Gauguin in 1875 (Musée d'Orsay, Paris), and the light-glittering river which Monet, Renoir, Alfred Sisley, and even Edouard Manet were already discovering at Argenteuil. In 1875, an article in "Paris-Journal," referring to the Impressionist sale on March 24, mentioned "violet countrysides, red flowers, black rivers, yellow or green women, and blue children." This was very different from the vision then offered by Gauguin. At the Salon des Indépendants in 1881 and 1882, Huysmans noted the Degas-like terse naturalism of Gauguin's *Study of a Nude* or *Suzanne Sewing* (see page 11) — "No one ever gave such vehement note to reality" — but he also commented on the dull tones, "sickly and muted colors" of his *Studio*. Even at the eighth and last Impressionist exhibition in 1886, Félix Fénéon's sharp eye was struck by Gauguin's "muted harmony," insisting on its heavy, almost sodden nature: "Dense trees shoot up from a heavy, rich, and damp soil."

THE BIRTH OF A NEW ART

Around 1885, Gauguin's great venture started, with its poverty, wandering, and the slow conquest of genius. Already in 1885, when he was in Denmark trying to support his family by selling tarpaulin, and when his painting was still struggling in the limbo of a dull Impressionism, he clearly perceived an art which he was to shape only a few years later. His letter to Emile Schuffenecker, dated January 14, 1885, confirms this. Gauguin was not the sport of irresistible impulses rising from the depth of his inner sensations; he viewed creation as the consequence of thought.

Portrait of Madeleine Bernard, 1888.   Oil on canvas, 28⅜″ × 22⅞″ (72 × 58 cm)
Musée des Beaux-Arts, Grenoble

Four Breton Girls Dancing, 1886
Oil on canvas, 28⅜″ × 35⅞″ (72 × 91 cm)
Bayerische Staatsgemäldesammlungen
Neue Pinakothek, Munich

VISION OF THE SERMON
(JACOB WRESTLING WITH THE ANGEL), 1888
Oil on canvas, 28¾″ × 36¼″ (73 × 92 cm)
National Gallery, Edinburgh

BRETON BOYS BATHING, 1888.   Oil on canvas, 36¼″ × 28¾″ (92 × 73 cm)
Kunsthalle, Hamburg

His career as a painter and the cycle of his escapes really started at this time. In 1886, he stayed for the first time in Brittany, at the Gloanec boarding-house in Pont-Aven; it was the beginning of his friendship with Emile Bernard, whom he met in Brittany, and Van Gogh, whom he met in Paris. In 1887, he escaped for the first time across the seas, with the painter Charles Laval, and made his first exotic experiments in Panama and Martinique, returning to Paris in December. In 1888, he stayed a second time at Pont-Aven, where a new and decisive meeting with Bernard brought forward a new doctrine about painting. At the same time, Gauguin became an influential member, even the leader of a group. His first one-man exhibition was held at the Boussod & Valadon gallery, where Van Gogh's brother, Theo, worked. Young painters began to regard him as the master of pictorial symbolism and rallied around him. In October 1888, Gauguin went to Arles on Van Gogh's invitation, to try

Breton Woman Seen from the Back, 1886
Pastel
Art Gallery and Museum, Glasgow
Burrell Collection

and build up an artists' community which Van Gogh had long dreamed to create. The idea was to change the material and moral circumstances of artists, to bring into existence "a studio for a renaissance and not for decadence," as Van Gogh wrote to his brother Theo before Gauguin arrived. "In our association, each of us will be more himself, while union also means strength." Gauguin arrived on October 20. By December 25, all hopes had vanished, all plans were annihilated. There was the often told tragedy, Van Gogh's abortive murderous attempt, when he slashed his own ear. Gauguin fled without ever seeing again his tempestuous friend, who was always to feel bitter about this. By the end of 1888 Gauguin was back in Paris, where, more than ever, he was regarded as the forerunner of a new aesthetic movement, especially after the exhibition held at the Café Volpini on the occasion of the World Fair. In April 1889 he returned to Pont-Aven; but in October he preferred to settle in Melle Henry's inn at Le Pouldu, a more isolated village. One after the other, he produced such works

THE YELLOW CHRIST, 1889.   Oil on canvas, 36¼″ × 28⅞″ (92 × 73 cm)
The Albright-Knox Art Gallery, Buffalo, New York

THE GREEN CHRIST OR THE CALVARY, 1889.   Oil on canvas, 36¼″ × 28¾″ (92 × 73 cm)
Musées Royaux des Beaux-Arts de Belgique, Brussels

as *The Yellow Christ* (see page 34), *The Green Christ or The Calvary* (see page 35), *La Belle Angèle* (see page 41), which showed that, at last, he was in full possession of his art, with an equally masterful control of vision, plastic form, and technique. He stayed in Paris from December 1890 to the spring of 1891, and was honored at a dinner held at the Café Voltaire. On April 4, he set off for Tahiti again, for a final twelve-year period during which his destiny and art were fulfilled.

During these few years Gauguin had already come out of his first phase of mere, almost passive observation. He had become aware of the possibilities of technique. His shapes kept something of the compact, earthy power that he had borrowed from Pissarro and Millet. The example of Cézanne — like him, a man of a few words — had helped him to free his brushstroke. From then on, Gauguin wanted his brushstroke to be tight and even, applied in parallel, as if obstinate, hatching. This arbitrary technique helped him to distance himself from a direct imitation of reality and to become conscious of the independence of painting. In turn, his line broke free: It extended, unwinding and unbroken, and became a contour. He was helped by the firmness of the trees, design of branches, and trunks, and also by Cézanne's example. Above all, however, he was influenced by the works of Pierre Puvis de Chavannes and Japanese prints. The latter, especially, provided him with a model for an art attracted by the decorative effect, in which the artist respected the picture's surface, refusing to break it by false perspective and modeling and preferring to rely on unfolding lines and flat areas of color. Like the Japanese printmakers, Gauguin did not sacrifice line and color for the sake of imitation and trompe-l'oeil but, as a counterpart, he had to heighten their suggestive power. He did not develop only the possibilities of the line as an arabesque, but also its expressive equivalences. Thereby,

Breton Boy, ca 1888
Charcoal and red pencil on paper
19½″ × 13¾″ (49.5 × 34.9 cm)
Private Collection
Courtesy Robert Schmit Gallery, Paris

Gauguin announced Henri de Toulouse-Lautrec, who was to seek also in the works of Puvis de Chavannes and the Japanese printmakers the secret of this double aspect of the line.

A painter's surroundings are always revealing. Seguin told us that Gauguin had hung reproductions on the walls of his studio at Le Pouldu. They all reflected his preoccupation with bringing out the continuity and harmony of drawing. There was Manet's *Olympia*, and one must remember the well-known comments on Manet's painting for "playing cards" as well as the significance he gave to contours. There were also the lissome works of Italian masters: Fra Angelico's *Annunciation* and Sandro Botticelli's *Spring*. Finally, there were decorations by Puvis de Chavannes and some prints by Utamaro.

Head of Peasant Girl
8⅞″ × 7⅞″ (22.4 × 20 cm)
The Fogg Art Museum, Harvard University
Cambridge, Massachusetts
Collection Meta and Paul J. Sachs

He knew Puvis de Chavannes and had had conversations with him. In 1898, he still put him on the list of the great artists whom he wanted invited to his exhibition. In 1901, he copied Puvis's *Hope* in the background of a still life (former Nathan Cummings Collection). He often mentioned Japanese art, as did most of the Impressionists, and he included Japanese prints in some paintings, as in *The Schuffenecker Family* (see page 42).

More than Puvis de Chavannes, Japanese prints prompted him to use flat areas of intense color. When he first tried exoticism, when he escaped from poverty and sought the unknown by going to Martinique in 1887, he was bitterly disappointed, but he discovered at least the density of tones under more luminous skies. From this time on, his colors were more and more definite; they were intensely bright, never light or flickering. His inner solemnity kept him separate from the Impressionists' liveliness. When he went back to Brittany in 1888, his style asserted itself, attracted notice, became even provocative. Nature was definitely tamed and had no say; it submitted meekly to the imperious transmutation which forced it out of its three dimensions into the two dimensions of the picture's surface, where line and color could follow their

Breton Women
in Front of a Fence, 1889
Zincograph
6¹¹/₁₆″ × 8⁷/₁₆″ (17 × 21.5 cm)
Bibliothèque nationale, Paris

own law.   Gauguin knew it.   "I do not paint from life," he wrote to Emmanuel Bibesco in 1900, "today less than ever."   In the same year, the new generation's spokesman, Maurice Denis, wrote a now famous article in "L'Occident" and he acknowledged that, during the days of Pont-Aven, Gauguin "freed us from all the chains with which the idea of copying [nature] had bound our artistic instincts."   From that time on, a modern aesthetic movement was born, with all its boldness and possibilities.

Was Gauguin truly the author of such revolution?   Emile Bernard never ceased to protest and deny it, for which Gauguin was to remain bitterly resentful.   Who was the initiator, Gauguin or Bernard?   Who coined the word "synthesis" in this context, which Gauguin — who hated theories — spelled "*saintaise*, because it rhymes with *foutaise* (nonsense)"?[1]   Historians have debated the problem and come to different conclusions.   One thing is certain: Even before meeting Bernard — "the young Bernard" who was only twenty-four years old and whom he welcomed as would a master already surrounded by disciples — Gauguin was progressing steadily toward the affirmation of the power of line and color, freed from the direct imitation of nature.   It is also certain that the new doctrine did not bring about anything that had not been achieved in the Japanese prints that Gauguin loved.   Finally, in his letter

(1) While being so sensitive to thought, Gauguin was highly suspicious of theories and the artificial molds which they forced upon creativity.   Although a Symbolist himself, he made fun of the Symbolist movement and its dogmatism. Daniel de Monfreid told of Gauguin's knowing smile, approving of Paul Verlaine who exclaimed ironically at the Café Voltaire, "Oh bother!   How they bore me, these cymbalists!»

to Schuffenecker dated January 14, 1885, Gauguin had already formulated his theory of the symbolically expressive power of color and line, which implied that he was aware that they could be used freely regardless of their representational value. It is also certain, however, that Gauguin's dreamy and uncommunicative nature always proceeded gradually, leaning on whatever support it found in outside events. He had neither the dogmatic mind nor the confidence that Bernard was to develop later and which were to drive him to repudiations and extreme positions.

Anyway, how significant was an influence on a great man like Gauguin? It brought no more that the revelation of a form in which he could inscribe that which he already carried in his soul and for which he was seeking expression. Gauguin

Portrait of Stéphane Mallarmé, 1891
Etching, 7⅛″ × 5⅝″ (18.2 × 14.3 cm)
Collection Manoukian, Paris

knew that Bernard had not brought him anything that he did not have already and to which he had not given some thought. Bernard could note that on such and such a day, at such and such an hour, he had proposed a "system" for painting, by which Gauguin's aspirations had suddenly found a suitable form. The quarrel is pointless. Bernard did not change Gauguin's destiny as a painter, but he gave him the syntax needed for his language. The only thing that matters is that which Gauguin handed us down.

THE SYMBOLIST DOCTRINE

In any event Gauguin knew where he was heading for, at least since 1885, when he wrote from Denmark to Schuffenecker on January 14 and May 24. While he was entering a phase of uncertainty in his painting, he could nevertheless formulate already the program of Symbolism. He fully appreciated the bewildering novelty of this program, and it upset him. "I feel sometimes as though I were crazy," he wrote in

Breton Women, ca 1892
Pastel, 11¹³/₁₆" × 16½" (30 × 42 cm)
Private collection

the first of these letters. He had discovered that aside from having the power to reproduce that which we see — the reality shown by nature's appearance — line and color have also an emotional power that can convey a mood to the viewer. "There are noble lines, false lines.... A straight line suggests infinity, a curved line limits creativity.... Colors explain still more.... Some tones are noble, some vulgar, some harmonies suggest tranquility, consolation, some excite you into doing something bold." This was also valid for shapes. In an orchestrated art, "the most intimate part of man is veiled." This was a most significant remark, because it contained all of Symbolism, predating the writings of Emile Bernard and Georges-Albert Aurier.

Therefore, was Gauguin the inventor of Symbolism? Let us not be rash! There were surprising connections between his observations and the theories of both Charles Baudelaire and Eugène Delacroix, who had instilled into Baudelaire his ideas on art. In his second draft of a preface for the "Flowers of Evil," Baudelaire explained that "the poetic phrase can imitate ... a horizontal line, an ascending or descending vertical line; ... it can rise straight up to heaven without losing its breath, or go perpendicularly to hell with the velocity of any weight." He added, "Poetry is like the art of painting ... in its ability to express every sensation of sweetness or bitterness, beatitude or horror." [1] In his "Curiosités Esthétiques" he had perceived that Delacroix's works made use of this mysterious power: "The wonderful chords

(1) "Three Drafts of a Preface," in *The Flowers of Evil.* Tr. by Jackson Mathews. New York: New Directions, 1955, pp. XIII-XIV.

LA BELLE ANGÈLE, 1889.   Oil on canvas, 36″ × 28⅖₁₆″ (91.5 × 72.5 cm)
Musée d'Orsay, Paris

The Schuffenecker Family, 1889
Oil on canvas
28¾″ × 36¼″ (73 × 92 cm)
Musée d'Orsay, Paris

The Cellist - Portrait of Upaupa Schneklud, 1894
Oil on canvas, 36½″ × 28⅞″ (92.5 × 73.5 cm)
Museum of Art, Baltimore
Gift of H. K. Blaustein in memory of J. Blaustein

43

PORTRAIT OF A YOUNG GIRL, VAÏTÉ GOUPIL, 1896. Oil on canvas, 29½″ × 25⅝″ (75 × 65 cm)
Ordrupgaardsamlingen, Charlottenlund-Copenhagen. Collection Wilhelm Hansen

of his color often lead one to dream of harmony and melody." Similarly, Gauguin wrote in his letter, "A deep feeling can immediately be translated: Dream over it and seek its simplest shape." He elaborated on the emotional quality of shapes and specified that this quality belonged to the realm of sensations. Everything is contained in this single word: sensations. They are expressed before thoughts, conveying, by their own means and independently from thoughts, "the most delicate and therefore least visible emanations of the brains ... every human feeling." Similar ideas were taking shape wherever Baudelaire left his mark, be it in the works of Odilon Redon or Gustave Moreau, who claimed, "The evocation of thought through line, arabesque, and pictorial means, that is my aim." [1]

Gauguin went on pondering and, on May 24, he clarified the consequences of his discovery and, above all, art's opposition to realism, which had appeared until then as art's main function: "Nothing but painting, no trompe-l'oeil." The

Young Girl (detail), ca 1888
Charcoal and watercolor
13½″ × 9¾″ (34.2 × 24.7 cm)
Private collection
Courtesy Robert Schmit Gallery, Paris

purpose of drawing is less to imitate reality than to express the message contained in a work. "The line ... is a means to emphasize an idea." It is worth noting that here Gauguin joined Maurice Denis, who was to write in "Théories": "I persist in believing that it was innovative to stop reproducing life and nature through approximations and improvised trompe-l'oeils, and to reproduce our emotions and dreams through harmonious shapes and colors." As early as in the beginning of 1885, Gauguin made "ideas" the purpose of art rather than the representation of nature. Three years later, Aurier stated in the "Mercure de France" that from now on "a work of art

(1) Larger black notebook, p. 39. Archives, Musée Gustave Moreau, Paris. Tr. by James Emmous.

WOMAN IN THE WAVES, 1889
Oil on canvas
36¼″ × 28⁵⁄₁₆″ (92 × 72 cm)
The Cleveland Museum of Art
Gift of Mr. and Mrs. William Powell Jones

NIRVANA: PORTRAIT OF MEYER DE HAAN, ca 1890
Oil thinned with turpentine on silk
8″ × 11½″ (20.3 × 29.2 cm)
Wadsworth Atheneum, Hartford, Connecticut
Collection E. G. Sumner and M. C. Sumner

Study for The Loss of Virginity, 1890-1891
Charcoal, 12⁷⁄₁₆" × 13⅛" (31.6 × 33.2 cm)
Private collection

would be ideaistic, as its sole ideal will be to express Ideas."

Aside from this issue of priority of claim, which could lead to some bitterness, a new concept of art was to take hold of minds and works during these few years before 1890. In 1886, Paris saw the arrival of Van Gogh, who emerged right away from the cocoon of his early style, while Gauguin settled at Pont-Aven in Brittany, freeing himself from early influences and inventing "Synthetism." Later the public would discover at the Café Volpini, on the occasion of the World Fair of 1889, the new school which had formed around Gauguin. It definitely repudiated Impressionism, even taking the opposite course, and it joined forces with Symbolism in literature. 1884-1889, five years had elapsed between the Salon des Indépendants and the Café Volpini — a complete overturn had taken place.

At the same time, literature was going through a similar revolution, a similar need to break with the past and escape from tradition. In 1885, René Ghil opened fire by publishing his "Traité du Verbe"; the next year he founded the Ecole Symbolique et Humaniste, and Jean Moréas published his manifesto on Symbolism in "Le Figaro." Favorable influences were converging at the same time: In 1884 E.M. De Voguë introduced the Russian novel in France; in 1885 the "Revue Wagnérienne" was first published. Around the same period, there was a proliferation of anti-naturistic reviews: 1884, the subversive "Revue Indépendante" and Maurice Barrès's "Les Taches d'Encre"; 1886, "Pléiade," "Vogue" — which featured poems by Jules Laforgue — "Symbolisme" published by Gustave Kahn and Jean Moréas, "Décadent," and "Décadence"; 1889 — the year of the exhibition at the Café Volpini — "Plume" and "Mercure de France" first appeared. This was also the time when Paul Verlaine settled in Paris and published his "Art Poétique," Stéphane Mallarmé opened his salon, J.-K. Huysmans published "A Rebours," and Jules Laforgue "Complaintes."

THE LOSS OF VIRGINITY (AWAKENING OF SPRING), 1891
Oil on canvas, 35⅜″ × 51¼″ (90 × 130 cm)
The Chrysler Museum of Art, Norfolk, Virginia. Gift of Walter P. Chrysler Jr.

From then on, and for fifteen years, Gauguin set out to change the traditional basis of art, with a fierce and stubborn energy and a growing solitude far from civilization. He disclosed possibilities in art which are still being explored nowadays. Amidst pain, poverty, and adversity, he was to break the shackles that bound him and his contemporaries and bring freedom to the art of the future. By the end of the century, he had forebodings of that which was being accomplished: "I think that despite the number of clever characters and frauds, this coming century will bring quite a beautiful crop in art." Proudly, he already reckoned what this art would owe him: "Martyrdom is often necessary for a revolution. Considered as an immediate result," he added modestly, "my work is of little significance compared to the final and moral result: Painting is freed of all its chains, of this dreadful amalgamation woven by schools, academies, and, above all, mediocrities."[1]

TAHITI AND THE QUEST FOR ORIGINS

Gauguin left Paris in the spring of 1891, in a new venture in the spirit of his unsuccessful trip to Martinique and his first attempt to escape a world rotten by civilization. This time he had decided to go further in quest of the mirage of man's origins and purity,

(1) To Dr. Gouzer, March 15, 1898.

Seated Maori Figure
Pen and ink
Musée de Rouen

in the South Seas. "On June 8," he noted,[1] "after sixty-three days of crossing, sixty-three days of feverish waiting, we saw strange fires zig-zagging on the sea." It was fragrant Tahiti, *Noa Noa*, the delightful land of Tahiti, *Nave Nave Fenua*. But the small provincial capital, Papeete, showed him nothing but a ridiculous imitation of the civilization which had already preceded him over there and which he had rejected. "An absurd, almost caricatural imitation of our customs, fashions, vices, and civilized futilities.... To have traveled so far to find this, this from which I was running away!" So Gauguin left one morning in a car borrowed from an officer; he drove for twenty-nine miles and settled down in Mateïea district. "On one side the sea, on the other the mountain.... Between the mountain and the sea, there is a cabin in burao wood.... Between the sky and me, nothing but the large, tall fragile roof, made out of pandanus leaves, where lizards hide."

Maori Woman with Hat
Lead pencil on beige paper
5⅞" × 4¼" (15 × 10.8 cm)
Musée de Rouen

Soon, however, loneliness bore in upon Gauguin; he had made friends with the neighbors, but,

> In the shade of the pandanus leaves
> You know that it is good to love.

One day he went on a search throughout the island, in the mountains, throughout the valleys. He trotted to the eastern coast on a horse borrowed from a gendarme. In Fanoe, he was invited to stop and eat: "You seek a wife? Do you want my daughter?" asked the Maori woman. Fifteen minutes later she came back with a "tall child, graceful

(1) This quote and the ones that follow are from *Noa Noa*.

51

STREET IN TAHITI, 1891.   Oil on canvas, 45½″ × 34⅞″ (115.5 × 88.5 cm)
The Toledo Museum of Art, Ohio

and slender." This was Tehura. "This child, about thirteen years old (corresponding to 18 to 20 in Europe) both charmed and awed me, she almost frightened me." They went back to Mateïea. "Then started a fully happy life." Tehura led him gradually to "a full comprehension of her race," through life's daily teaching. "Thanks to her I am beginning to grasp a number of mysteries which had remained incomprehensible to me."

Gauguin was about to try an extraordinary experiment and cast off the old European man, breaking off with the aesthetic criteria, inspiration, and style of a gradually ossified civilization, "this deceptive and conventional European civilization." He went back to the sources, where he hoped to recover man's truth. This is usually regarded as a supreme effort to escape, brought about by an exasperated individualism, a desire to break off with acquired and passively respected traditions,

Head of a Young Man. Left Profile, n.d.
Crayon with white and color highlights
18⅛″ × 13″ (46 × 33 cm)
Private collection
Courtesy Robert Schmit Gallery, Paris

a personality eager for freedom striving toward liberation and independence. This may not be quite accurate. Modern man has asserted more and more strongly the rights of his conscience and lucidity, his independence, his aptitude to conceive and direct himself by his own logic. In so doing he has severed gradually his links with his community; he has become uprooted, not only from his native soil but also from humanity. The modern malaise, with its crisis of sated individualism and its instinctive return to collective passivity, might be only obscure gropings of man to pull himself together and recover his connection with a nourishing trunk. On closer analysis, this was Gauguin's instinctive quest. Modern civilized society seemed no longer capable of fulfilling its regenerating and nourishing role; it could create only conflicts. Gauguin rejected "the horses of the Parthenon," wanting to return to "the rocking horse of his childhood." He aspired to recover man in his yet undamaged state, a spring

not yet dried up that would dispense the vital nourishment from which man seemed to have been prematurely weaned.

The whole first half of our century endeavored to destroy rationalism and replace it by "a quiet submission to that which the unconscious brings," as Redon put it. Liberalism was shaken and replaced by planning; collective imperatives, however blind, were upheld against individual freedom. The social structure was to be reshaped along those lines. This may be the reaction and fate of a world swept by excessive experiments toward individualism and trying to surge back in the opposite direction. Here again a precursor, Gauguin was already perturbed by all this. Therefore he perceived that which civilized man calls contemptuously *barbarian* and *savage* as morally wholesome, as containing a primordial purity, a healthier and more normal state of human condition. This idea haunted him. So he escaped always further, first to Brittany, and then to Martinique, Tahiti, the Marquesas Islands.

Before Pablo Picasso and André Derain discovered African art, Gauguin found his inspiration in primitive arts. In 1887, at Martinique, he was still faithful to the more or less Impressionistic naturalism of his beginnings; clearly, he was not influenced by any local art. In 1888, in Brittany, he took the plunge and renounced realism, helped by Emile Bernard's doctrinal formulation and the influence of Japanese prints. From this time on, his canvases were mainly a careful arrangement of line and color. The danger, however, was to create a purely decorative painting. Toward the end of his stay in Brittany, in 1889, the ancient Breton calvaries gave a soul to his emerging style and to a form which would have drifted otherwise toward Art Nouveau. A fierce, primitive soul, a sacred presence and its mystery, came back to life in the midst of a decadent realism. Let us compare two paintings produced around that time, *Breton Boys Bathing* (1888, see page 32) and *The Green Christ or The Calvary* (1889, see page 35): The plastic form and arrangement, which was already emerging from Naturalism, is transformed; it is struck by a religious solemnity, a perception of an unknown god that was to lead Gauguin in his quest for the primitive soul which he wanted to renew in himself. Things sacred are present in the background of his portraits, which he wanted to put in expressive harmony with the faces, according to the Symbolist doctrine which inspired also Van Gogh. In 1890, he placed *The Yellow Christ* in background of a self-portrait (Private collection). Strange anguished faces are whirling around Meyer de Haan in *Nirvana* (see page 47). He did not refer only to Christianity and Bhuddism, which he mentioned often in his writings. He was less attracted by dogmas than by the impact of things sacred, the meaning of which our time, even our religion, had lost. He regarded things sacred as linked with a darkly virgin and barbaric power. The Idol was to bring him that which God no longer gave him.

THE BARBARIC SOURCES

Gauguin had already placed the first of his idols, motionless and mysterious, near the *Belle Angèle* (see page 41). What is it? He no doubt was inspired by the Chimu pottery of the northwest coast of Peru and its stirrup portrait vases. Some vases from the Chancay valley are somewhat similar in shape. Gauguin himself said about himself that there was something "savage" in him. His grandmother was the famous Flora Tristan, born in Peru, the daughter of Don Mariano Tristan y Moscoso, a Spanish colonel

Title page of the journal
Le Sourire, 1899
Woodcut on Japan paper
4¹/₁₆" × 7³/₁₆" (10.3 × 18.2 cm)
Collection David Grob

serving in Lima, and the niece of a viceroy. His great-aunt was married in Bogota, Columbia, into the Uribe family. "There are two natures in me," Gauguin wrote to his wife in 1888, "an Indian and a sensory nature." And he tried to light again the spark of primitivism out of the ashes of his unconscious. In 1851, when he was three years old, he was taken to Peru by his father, who died during the trip. He spent four years in Lima with his mother and sister. One can imagine the deep and terrifying impression the Mochica vases — which were everywhere, even in his home — must have made on him and how his childhood questions and fantasies — the seeds of his adult questions and fantasies — took hold of these shapes. An obscure attraction, the magic of childhood's memories brought him back to these strange and doubly fascinating images. "The gods of yesteryear have kept a sanctuary in the memory of women," he wrote one day, but they have also done so in the memory of children.

There is definite evidence from Gauguin himself that he was familiar with these Peruvian vases. He noted in "Avant et Après," "My mother had kept some Peruvian vases and also a number of figures made of solid silver, pure silver as it comes out of the mines.

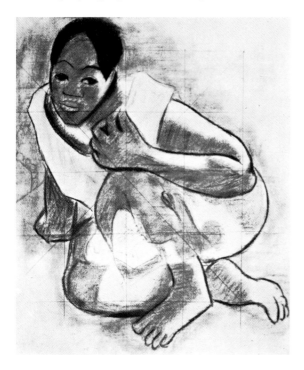

Crouching Tahitian Girl, 1891-1892
Charcoal and pastel
21¾" × 18¾" (55.3 × 47.8 cm)
The Art Institute, Chicago
Gift of Tiffany and Mrs. Margaret Blake

It all disappeared in the fire at Saint-Cloud which the Prussians had set." So he grew up and lived until the age of twenty-three surrounded by these strange artifacts. He found some more at the house of Père Maury, a French industrialist who had made a fortune in Lima by providing its cemetery with the Italian craftsmen's surplus production of pompous funeral monuments. "I saw again the old Père Maury," he wrote, "He had a very nice collection of vases (Inca pottery) and lots of jewels in unalloyed gold made by the Indians."

In 1889, an event helped Gauguin to focus his curiosity. He was already watched by the "evil spirit," but the Peruvian vases and their somewhat good-natured realism did not suffice to give it a shape. The World Fair — on the occasion of which the

NAFEA FAA IPOIPO. WHEN WILL YOU MARRY? 1892. Oil on canvas, 40″ × 30½″ (101.5 × 77.5 cm)
Collection Rudolf Staechelin, Basel

VAHINE NO TE VI. WOMAN WITH MANGO, 1892
Oil on canvas, 28⅝″ × 17½″ (72.7 × 44.5 cm)
The Baltimore Museum of Art, Maryland. The Cone Collection

FAATURUMA. THE DREAMER, 1891
Oil on canvas, 37″ × 26¾″ (73 × 92 cm)
The Nelson-Atkins Museum of Art, Kansas City, Missouri. The Nelson Fund

Nave Nave Fenua (Delicious Earth), ca 1891
Black and white woodcut
14⅛″ × 8³⁄₁₆″ (35.9 × 20.7 cm)
Musée des Arts africains et océaniens, Paris
Gift of Lucien Vollard

public could discover the Synthetism of Gauguin and his friends at the Café Volpini exhibition — brought to Gauguin a set of pre-Colombian works, mostly casting of Mexican art. He studied them carefully and made a number of drawings. He also studied the art of decorative scripts, especially Maya, in which straight perpendicular lines made designs resembling disorganized fragments of Greek frets. This aesthetic vision was entirely different from the European one and it prepared him for the somewhat related one that Tahiti was to offer. Similarly, he learned from the Zapotec art some simplified treatment of the human face, in which he indicated eyes and mouth with an almond shape crossed by a horizontal line.

When Gauguin landed in Tahiti in 1891, his memory carried already a stock of *barbaric* shapes. How much would he find there? There was no metal to make tools, no clay for pottery! Carved wood and painted cloth were the only vehicle for artistic creation. Moreover, the Polynesian pantheon is not very anthropomorphic. Taaroa and the gods descended from him remain symbols of the universe, earth, and heaven. The elevated Polynesian religion did not deem it necessary to represent them. In the west, in Samoa and Tonga, decorations were geometric. In the east, from the Hawaiian to the Society Islands — including the Marquesas Islands, where Gauguin eventually died — there are some effigies of gods. Art does not dare represent the supreme god, however, and it is limited to *Tiki*, stylized images of the male, fertilizing principle, which could be found on the handles of working implements as well as in stone statues. According to the tradition, these statues could be sixteen feet tall, like the statues on Easter Island, but there were only small ones when Gauguin arrived in Tahiti. J.A. Moerenhout published a very complete study of the South Seas Islands,[1] in which he wrote that the *Atuas* were set among the superior gods and had their stone or wooden images placed at the top of the *Maraes*, or temples which were mentioned by Gauguin. Aside from these images, called *Toas*, there were images of *Tiis*, or secondary gods, which were also described by Gauguin. These more carefully carved figures were erected along the temple's edges, as if to guard it, or on the shore, facing the sea. The huge mysterious statues on Eastern Island stand in a similar fashion; although it is still a matter for discussion, their significance seem to be explained by the ancient Tahitian custom. In his "Ancien Culte Mahorie," Gauguin mentioned these statues and noted their huge size. On the strength of this tradition, and in spite of the fact that he never actually saw a carved *Tii*, he may have felt that he could elaborate on the small statues which he

Head of a Tahitian Woman, 1891
Black pencil, 12¼" × 9⁷/₁₆" (31 × 24 cm)
The Cleveland Museum of Art
Collection Mr. and Mrs. Louis B. Williams

saw, and imagine them enlarged to monumental proportions in his paintings. He never actually saw the enormous, monstrous, and stupid idol, head drawn back into shoulders and hands folded over stomach, which he painted in many Tahitian scenes (see page 66). He thought it justified, however, to draw this idol from the small and middle-sized effigies that can be seen now at the Musée de l'Homme in Paris.

Gauguin's exoticism, therefore, implied less imagination than is usually supposed. His sometimes oddly stylized eyes and hands resemble that of the *Tikis*. They were constantly used to decorate the most common objects and finally evolved to simple geometric lines. We know that Gauguin studied them closely: The manuscript of "Noa Noa" includes pasted pieces of tracing paper, pencil rubbings of the raised engraved surface of decorated objects.[2] They show elements of *Tikis*: heads, silhouettes with

(1) *Voyages aux îles du Grand Océan*, 2 vols. Paris, 1837.
(2) *Noa Noa*, pp. 168-169.

61

arms folded over the stomach, and the simplified shape that Gauguin used for the hands of his gods. Unlike his statues, his paintings of cloths did not follow any regular decorative arrangement. There again, Gauguin was accurate. Polynesian cloth, the *Tapa*, was made from bark's inner fibers pounded with a grooved mallet, and its decoration was much less abstract. It was decorated with the imprints of plants, briars, or objects that had been dipped into red or yellow dye extracted from tree barks and pressed on the cloth. To create his barbarian gods, Gauguin did not only seek inspiration in his pre-Colombian memories — which had prepared him for the arts of the South Seas; he also studied Polynesian art carefully, whether representational or stylized.

When Gauguin returned to France in August 1893, penniless and sick, he settled in a studio at 4 Rue Vercingétorix, in Paris, with Annah the Javanese, a mulatto whom he had found wandering in the street and who soothed his nostalgia for faraway lands and races. According to his friend Paco Durrio, he decorated his new abode with numerous Polynesian works, which he had brought back, especially idols "carved in unknown red, orange, or black woods."[1]

THE LAST STAY IN THE SOUTH SEAS

Gauguin had a last meeting with his wife in Copenhagen at the beginning of 1894. The following April, he went back to Brittany, first to Pont-Aven, then to Le Pouldu.

---

(1) F. Cossio del Pomar, "La Vida de Pablo Gauguin." Introduction to the catalogue of a retrospective exhibition, Association Paris-Amérique latine, Paris, December 1926.

He broke his ankle at Concarneau, in a stupid fight about Annah, whom he had taken along. He came back to Paris in December and decided to return to Tahiti. After a disastrous auction sale of his works at the Hôtel Drouot on February 18, 1895, he set off for the Fragrant Island. Disappointment was awaiting him again in the place of his dreams. A little more than two years later, in January 1898, he tried to commit suicide, which he had been contemplating for a few months. He was exhausted by solitude and poverty and felt betrayed by his wife, who thought only of selling the paintings which he was sending her, without ever allowing him any part of the proceeds. He was wounded to the depth of his soul by the news, in April 1897, that his favorite daughter, Aline, had died. Bankrupt and hard pressed, he was unable to reimburse that year's loan from the Caisse Agricole and feared foreclosure. He was sick, tortured by the pain in his leg, which never healed properly after the accident at Concarneau, and by a wasting eczema; his sight was impaired by a double conjunctivitis; his life was threatened by a badly treated syphilis. He was vomiting blood. How far he was now from the mirage of "Tahiti, delightful land!" He first mentioned suicide in June 1897. In December, his mind was set. With unbelievable courage, he decided to put the final touch to his work. He painted his declaration of artistic principles, the title of which calls to mind the scientist and philosopher Blaise Pascal, *Where Do We Come From? Who Are We? Where Are We Going?* (see pages 78-79). He worked at it "during the whole month ... night and day, with an incredible fever," and he dated his last entry in his book of records, January 1898. He took to the mountains, "where my body would have been devoured by ants," and swallowed a large dose of arsenic; but he took too much and was

Noa Noa (Fragrant Fragrant), 1893
Woodcut, 14¹¹/₁₆″ × 8¹/₁₆″ (35.7 × 20.4 cm)
Musée des Arts africains et océaniens, Paris
Gift of Lucien Vollard

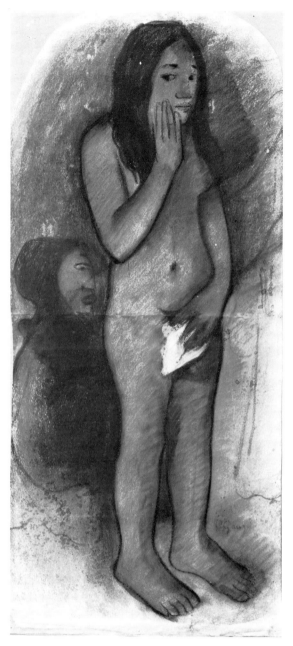

Words of the Devil (Eve), 1892
Pastel on paper, 30⁵/₁₆″ × 14″ (77 × 35.5 cm)
Kupferstichkabinett der öffentlichen
Kunstsammlung, Basel

sick to his stomach. This saved him and, "after a night of dreadful suffering," he went home.

Life went on and so did his work. In August 1901, Gauguin settled in the Marquesas Islands, in the remote village of Atuana, where he built his "house of Pleasure," decorated with his wood carvings and paintings. The lack of money and ill-health were made worse by a permanent, incessantly inflamed, conflict with the authorities, from the police to the bishop. In his dealings with the natives, and in "Le Sourire," the paper he both edited and illustrated, he induced them to rebel against the discipline imposed that destroyed slowly the soul of their ancient civilization. In the midst of these worries that gradually weakened him, he painted his last masterpieces, *And the Gold of Their Bodies* (1901, Musée d'Orsay, Paris), *Barbaric Tales* (see page 81). They followed the ones painted in Tahiti, the most famous of which are *Ia Orana Maria* (1891, The Metropolitan Museum of Art, New York), *Manao Tupapau. The Specter Watches over Her* (see page 68) — executed during his first stay in Tahiti — *Nevermore* (see page 76), *The White Horse* (see page 86), and *Two Tahitian Women* or *Tahitian Women with Mango Blossoms* (see page 82) — executed during his second stay there. On March 23, 1903, he was sentenced to a fine and jail for "having accused a gendarme." "All these worries are killing me," he wrote to his friend Monfreid. He was found dead on May 8. His posthumous life had started.

Parau Na Te Varaua Ino. Words of the Devil, 1892. Oil on canvas, 36⅛″ × 27″ (91.7 × 68.5 cm)
The National Gallery of Art, Washington, D.C.
Gift of the W. Averell Harriman Fund in the memory of Marie N. Harriman

Parahi Te Marae. There Is the Temple, 1892. Oil on canvas, 28¾″ × 35¾″ (68 × 91 cm)
The Philadelphia Museum of Art. Gift of Mrs. Rodolphe Meyer de Schauensee

Maruru (Thank You), 1891-1894
Woodcut, 2nd state
11″ × 18⅞″ (28 × 48 cm)
Musée des Arts africains et
océaniens, Paris

GAUGUIN AND THE CRISIS OF THE WESTERN WORLD

Beyond Gauguin, there is the problem of our civilization's evolution and of his place therein. It is a problem of civilization, which Gauguin formulated bluntly in 1895, in a letter to a great Western intellectual, August Strindberg. He felt "the whole impact between your civilization and my barbarism. You suffer from civilization. I am rejuvenated by barbarism." In the twilight of an aging civilization, Gauguin "the Savage from Peru," "the Indian," as he called himself, outlined ways through which this civilization can and will try to escape from itself, to break smothering boundaries. He perceived this conflict and defined it clearly. He rebelled against the existing ancient culture, against the Greek-Latin tradition which had created Europe but was dying of its own ossification. He was not alone in this rebellion, but his roots and genius made him express more clearly and categorically a malaise, which came to light with the Romantics and quickly grew since. Oswald Spengler wrote of "the decline of the West." Gauguin claimed his condemnation of the Latin culture. He was to repeat it over and again, as in a letter to Monfreid dated October 1897, "Always bear in mind things Persian, Cambodian, and even something of the Egyptians. [1] Things Greek are a great mistake, however beautiful they may be." What irked him in the works of Puvis de Chavannes, in spite of his admiration for him? "He is a Greek, while I am a savage, a collarless wolf from the woods." [2] No more Pegasus, no more horses of the Parthenon! One must go back, "far back, further than the horses of the Parthenon — as far as the rocking horse of my childhood, the good old wooden horse." [3] This

---

(1) The painting *Ta Matete, The Market* (1892, Kunstmuseum, Basel) is significant in that regard. Its figures seem Egyptian.
(2) This was Degas's sally. Gauguin was secretly flattered and repeated it often.
(3) *Avant et Après.*

MANAO TUPAPAU. THE SPECTER WATCHES OVER HER, 1892. Oil on canvas, 28¾″ × 36¼″ (73 × 92 cm)
The Albright-Knox Art Gallery, Buffalo, New York. Collection A. Conger Goodyear

was less of a sally than a message. Anyhow, "these blasted Greeks, who had understood everything," they taught that "animality which we carry in us should not be as despised as it is said," for "they conceived of Antaeus, who recovered his strength by touching the earth. Believe me, the earth is our animality!" This is our unconscious. Was it not time to renew the mythical Antaeus? Gauguin asked this question with his whole work.

This may have been the dominant problem of our time. For years we have witnessed our civilization's dramatic effort to reach beyond its own well organized thoughts, recover the primordial soil beyond an overly codified culture, and reach the unconscious that has become an obsession in literature, art, philosophy, psychology, and even medicine — in all of modern life. This passionate curiosity has carried us toward simpler arts, closer to their origins: primitive arts, whether African or archaic, children's drawings, works of the Sunday painters and the mentally ill. This may be a sign of the instinct and nostalgia that drive the modern world toward the origins of thoughts, in a search for regeneration. It knows that it must break the discipline of rationality, which is a corset that strengthened this world but stifled it once it started to grow.

Gauguin tried to identify this malaise through his art. "Primitive art," he stated, "comes from the mind and uses nature. The so-called refined art is borne from sensuality and serves nature. Nature is the servant of the former and the mistress of the latter.... Nature degrades the mind by letting itself be adored. This is how we fell into the awful mistake of Naturalism." In his opinion, this race toward Naturalism, which

Manao Tupapau
(The Specter Watches over Her), 1894
Black lithograph, pencil, pen, and wash
7⅛" × 10¹¹⁄₁₆" (18 × 27.1 cm)
Private collection, France

GRAPE GATHERING AT ARLES OR HUMAN MISERY, 1888
Oil on canvas, 28¾″ × 36¼″ (73 × 92 cm)
Ordrupgaardsamlingen, Charlottenlund-Copenhagen
Collection Wilhelm Hansen

PONT-AVEN, THE VILLAGE, 1894
Oil on canvas, 28¾″ × 36¼″ (73 × 92 cm)
Private collection
Courtesy Acquavella Galleries, New York

Nativity, ca 1902
Traced monotype on wove paper
23" × 17¾" (58.5 × 45 cm)
Musée des Arts africains et océaniens, Paris

enslaved the mind, started with the Greek-Roman civilization. "Naturalism started with the Greeks at the time of Pericles.... In our present misery, there is but one salvation: a clear and reasoned return to the beginnings," that is to say to "primitive arts." Gauguin's statements might lead to misunderstandings. Clearly, the Greeks in the days of Pericles safeguarded the mind and did not know the materialistic realism to which their later followers were to succumb. Gauguin, however, was almost accurate. After Pericles, Aristoteles and his concern for particular and experimental facts, as opposed to Plato's ideas, reshaped our world. His philosophy gave us our certainties and achievements, but also our shortcomings and limitations, which do not exist in many primitive or Eastern cultures.

From then on, the West endeavored to give a stable and universal, therefore objective, basis to knowledge. This was found in the outside world, which is the source common to all our sensations. For more safety, this outside world was considered primarily under its material and spatial aspects, which are easily observed and measured, outside of time which is constantly modifying its identity. Having defined a series of phenomena, it tried to establish constant relations of cause and effect between them, so as to provide an explanation for them, foresee their recurrence, and allow their imitation or improvement. The culture was thus based on objective elements, concrete facts, and logical connections, and it strived to limit itself therein. It smothered and rejected the rest, all these inner, subjective revelations that jeopardized the universality of both positivist reality and reason. This culture became heavier and more systematic during the Roman era. It was deeply shaken in the early Middle Age by the fall of the Roman Empire and the onrush of barbarian elements. After the thirteenth century, it gradually recovered its hegemony with the revival of Aristoteles's philosophy and the rise of a middle class. From then on, culture was solidly based on sensation and logic, reality and reason. Starting in the fifteenth century, bourgeois Positivism in the North and Latin Renaissance in the South

POÈMES BARBARES, 1896.   Oil on canvas, 25⅜″ × 18⅞″ (64.6 × 48 cm)
The Fogg Art Museum, Harvard University, Cambridge, Massachusetts. Collection Maurice Wertheim

No Te Aha Oe Riri? Why Are You Angry? 1896
Oil on canvas, 37½″ × 51¼″ (95.3 × 130.5 cm)
The Art Institute, Chicago
Collection Mr. and Mrs. Martin A. Ryerson

NEVERMORE, 1897.   Oil on canvas, 23⅝″ × 45⅝″ (60 × 116 cm)
Courtauld Institute Galleries, London. Courtauld Collection

introduced an increasing exactness, and experimental science became culture's expression and triumphant tool. The sense of beauty and harmony that had maintained Greece's balance and spirituality vanished gradually, and the unrestrained expression of the soul, by which Christendom had regenerated our era, became distorted. Whether harmony or faith, everything yielded to dogmatic rule. The nineteenth century saw the triumph of the bourgeoisie in Naturalism, which grew out of the Renaissance and Academicism. Reason coupled with reality became the only and absolute formula.

Already at the beginning of the nineteenth century, many a mind concerned itself with the withering and suffocation felt everywhere. After the rational Sensualism of the eighteenth century, one witnessed with dread the source of inner life and its replenishment dry out. The increasing barrenness of the Greek and Latin tradition was frightening, as it was becoming narrower by the day, more restricted under the bourgeois rule. Romanticism was a desperate effort to

Where Do We Come From?
Who Are We?
Where Are We Going? 1898
Study on squared tracing paper, watercolor
8¹/₁₆″ × 14¾″ (20.5 × 37.5 cm)
Musée des Arts africains et océaniens, Paris

WHERE DO WE COME FROM?
WHO ARE WE?
WHERE ARE WE GOING? 1897
Oil on canvas, 54¾″ × 147½″ (139 × 735 cm)
Museum of Fine Arts, Boston
Arthur Gordon Tompkins Fund

79

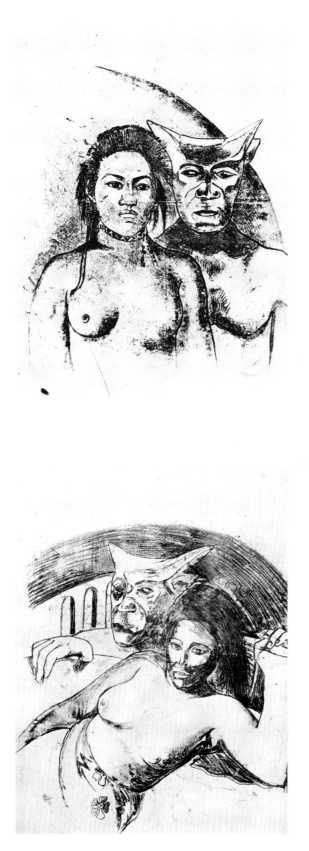

Tahitian Woman with Evil Spirit, ca 1900
Traced monotype, 25⅝″ × 18⅛″ (65 × 46 cm)
Private collection

break this choking circle, and a great effort was made to recover man's soul. Up to that time the most highly regarded arts were those relying on matter and space, such as sculpture and architecture. Such classical painting as that of the School of Jacques-Louis David aspired to imitate sculpture. As a reaction, Romantic painting turned to music, an art placed in time and outside of space, suggestive and no longer descriptive. In August 1901, Gauguin wrote to Daniel de Monfreid, "All told, painting should seek suggestion more than description, as does music." Time regained its significance, and so did the irrational, whether in literature, arts, or even science, to which this escape into irrationality gave an extraordinary development. Everything is conceived as a fleeting dynamic reality, resembling the principle of music. Color is closer to music than line, which is more spatial and rigid, and therefore color has become the main concern of modern painting.

Points of support had to be found to achieve this liberation. To escape from the narrowed Latin world, it became necessary to look beyond its frontiers. The time had

Tahitian Woman with Evil Spirit, ca 1900
Traced monotype on off-white, wove paper
20⁵⁄₁₆″ × 17⅞″ (56.1 × 45.3 cm)
Private collection

BARBARIC TALES, 1902.   Oil on canvas, 51⅛″ × 36¹⁄₁₆″ (130 × 89 cm)
Museum Folkwang, Essen

Two Tahitian Women, 1899. Oil on canvas, 37″ × 28½″ (94 × 72.4 cm)
The Metropolitan Museum of Art, New York. Gift of William Church Osborn

GIRL WITH A FAN, 1902.   Oil on canvas, 36¼″ × 28¾″ (92 × 73 cm)
Museum Folkwang, Essen

CROUCHING MARQUESAN WOMAN SEEN FROM THE BACK, ca 1902
Gouache monotype on buff laid paper, 21″ × 11⅛″ (53.2 × 28.3 cm)
Collection Mr. and Mrs. Eugene V. Thaw, New York

not yet come to turn to the South Seas as did Gauguin. This quest began with the Middle East, and, nearer still, the Northern and Germanic traditions, which, better than others, had kept safe from rationalism and realism — this was the hour of Shakespeare, Byron, and the German Romantics. One also went back in history, to periods that had known best how to free themselves from Rome, and the Middle Age was rediscovered. Gauguin brought this escape to its extreme limits with one stroke; in space, his quest took him to the antipodes, in time beyond all memory.

THE DISCOVERY OF MODERN SOUL

Another principle had to replace the one that was rejected. At the turn of the nineteenth century, Germany whispered the password of the new era, the beloved

Tahitian Woman with Evil Spirit (recto), ca 1900
Traced monotype on off-white, wove paper
25⅛″ × 20⅛″ (63.8 × 51.2 cm)
Städelsches Kunstinstitut, Francfort

Stimmung of the German poet Novalis, about which he said that "it indicates and announces states of the mind that are musical in nature." The *Stimmung*, or mood, atmosphere, was indeed the denial of rationalism, the first groping effort toward its enemy, the unconscious. The *Stimmung* is all that escapes definition, explanation, and their rigidity; it is all that is felt rather than understood, that belongs to the dark infinite realm of the soul rather than that of a clearly outlined rationality. From then on, art's goal was to depict the unique impulse to express our sensibility without restraint rather than apply definable rules of beauty.[1] Romanticism opened the way, and Gauguin became its heir, over and above the Realists' reaction against Romanticism. He broke free from rationalism and settled into the soul's dim, limitless, and exhilarating universe. "Night has come. All is quiet. I close my eyes *to see without understanding the dream of infinite space fleeing before me...*"[2]

(1) "Love that which will never be seen twice," said the poet Alfred de Vigny. What else did Impressionism do?
(2) Letter to André Fontainas, March 1899.

THE WHITE HORSE, 1898
Oil on canvas, 55½″ × 35⅞″ (141 × 91 cm)
Musée d'Orsay, Paris

BOUQUET OF FLOWERS, 1897
Oil on canvas, 28¾″ × 36⅝″ (73 × 93 cm)
Musée Marmottan, Paris.Duhem Bequest

Flight. The Ford. Tahitian on Horseback
ca 1902
Traced monotype on wove paper
19¹¹⁄₁₆″ × 17⁵⁄₁₆″ (50 × 44 cm)
Musée des Arts africains et océaniens, Paris

Dream and imagination as opposed to reality, time and its invisible dimension preferred to dull, motionless surfaces, the inexpressible to definition, the unknown and strange to certainties and principles, what else was there to break away from? The firmest basis of logic was the intangible principle of causality: To explain and understand everything through its cause and effect. The German Romantics, and later Delacroix and Baudelaire, outlined a play of analogies and connections, erecting a system of knowledge of the world, perceptions and explanations that they did not understand themselves, and which was similar to that of the primitive people and their magical approach to the world. Gauguin aspired to these relationships perceived by intuition and ignored by logic, these mystical links connecting one feeling to another, an appearance to an idea, nature to man, and weaving a web of inexpressible communion. He found them in Symbolism. To make sure, however, that these relationships would not be lost and degenerate into some fallacious literary doctrine, he sailed for primitive lands, where they ruled still, unpolluted by reason and its deductions. Delacroix had been the first in France to perceive this new system, and he planted the seeds. He opened Pandora's box, and elusive intoxicating fragrances spread into the air: all the new powers, intensity, imagination, color, music, correspondences, suggestions, and mystery.... Delacroix, however, had remained hampered: He was still a man steeped in classical culture and he thought more of reviving than of destroying tradition. He did not venture further. Gauguin was the first to become conscious of a break from which the modern world would emerge, the first to have escaped Latin, European civilization (as did Arthur Rimbaud, however) to find primordial impulses among barbaric tales and savage gods, the first to have lucidly repudiated and broken the law of reality and reason. Some have shaped modern art more directly, but no one has helped more the modern soul dare to be itself and follow a still unpredictable course. Western art was centered on that which was known, while Gauguin assigned it the task of

RIDERS ON THE BEACH, 1902. Oil on canvas, 26″ × 29¹⁵⁄₁₆″ (66 × 76 cm)
Museum Folkwang, Essen

Adam and Eve (Flight) -
Tahitian Couple Walking, ca 1900
Traced monotype on laid paper
20⅝" × 15⅝" (53 × 40 cm)
Private collection, France

expressing the unknown, toward which Rimbaud alone had launched his "Drunken Ship."

It would be pointless to wonder who was greater of Cézanne or Gauguin, Gauguin or Van Gogh. It might be said, however, that the voracity for discovering was stronger in Gauguin than a creativity surging from the depth of the being and forcing itself upon the world. He was less pushed forward by an inner urge than he was drawn incessantly by the never fulfilled mirage of the unknown. Throughout his life and development, Gauguin was in perpetual pursuit of an elsewhere. In this, he foreshadowed our own time, which is less aware of that which it wants than that it wishes to eschew. Gauguin expressed the modern soul, its impatient repudiations, its anxious avidity — in one word, its anguish — and he struck a chord that will always sound in man's heart.

When breaking free from sometimes questionable certainties, one is prepared to face emptiness; one discovers also the problem of destiny and its awesome grandeur. Gauguin is among the poets and artists who have lead us to the brink of our own enigma. Man has never been so assailed by the sharpness of this enigma as in the centuries when he has deliberately thrown down obsolete armors which no longer fit him. The nineteenth and twentieth centuries are such centuries.

In the nineteenth century Delacroix took pleasure in bending Hamlet's pallor and grief over Yorrick's silent skull. On the eve of the twentieth century, Gauguin went very far to find "in dreamy eyes the cloudy surface of a fathomless enigma." When he vainly sought death in attempted suicide, he put this enigma to us, in a painting in which three shattering cries demand an answer:

Where do we come from? Who are we? Where are we going?

BIOGRAPHY

1848 Eugène-Henri-Paul Gauguin was born on June 7, in Paris. His father, Clovis Gauguin, was a liberal journalist from Orléans. His mother, née Aline Chazal, was the daughter of Flora Tristan, a writer of Peruvian descent and a militant socialist.

1851 Clovis Gauguin embarked for Peru with his wife and two children. A republican and a political refugee, he hoped to start a new life in Peru with the help of his wife's influential relatives. He died on the way and was buried at Punta Arena, in the Straits of Magellan.

1851-1855 Madame Gauguin and her children stayed at the home of her uncle, Don Pio Tristan Moscoso, in Lima. Don Pio, a veteran of the war of independence in Peru and a very rich man, was the father-in-law of the president of the Republic, Jose Rufino Echenique.

1855 Responding to her dying father-in-law's request, Madame Gauguin took her family back to France. They settled at Orléans and lived with Gauguin's uncle, Isidore, who was also an opponent to Napoléon III's regime. The household owned a collection of Pre-Colombian art.

1859 Enrolled in a catholic boarding school at Orléans. His mother established herself as a seamstress in Paris.

1865 Failed the examination to enter the Navy and became an assistant pilot in the Merchant Marine. He traveled the Atlantic Ocean between Le Havre and Rio de Janeiro on the three-master Luzitano. An officer on board gave him a glowing account of the two years he had spent in Polynesia.

1866 Embarked as a second lieutenant on the larger three-master Chili.

1867 His mother died while Gauguin was at sea. She had appointed Gustave Arosa, a friend and an art collector, as a guardian to her children.

1868 Gauguin enlisted in the Navy in February.

1870 Outbreak of the Franco-Prussian war. Gauguin's ship, the Jérôme-Napoléon, saw combat in the North Sea. The family house at Saint-Cloud, near Paris, and its Pre-Colombian collection were destroyed by bombing.

1871 Outbreak of the Paris revolution, the Commune, which was defeated in May, after a "bloody week" of combat. Gauguin resigned from the Navy in April. Arosa helped him to find a job on the Paris Stock Exchange with the firm Bertin. There he met Emile Schuffenecker.

1872 Made a considerable fortune.

1873 Was leading the life of a well-to-do bourgeois. Took up painting with Schuffenecker in his spare time, in a style reminiscent of Corot's. Arosa introduced him to the works of the Impressionists. On November 22, Gauguin married Mette-Sophie Gaad, from Denmark, whom he had met the previous spring.

1874 Opening on April 15 of the first Impressionist group exhibition, at Nadar's studio, in which Manet refused to take part. Gauguin enrolled as a student in the studio of Colarossi. Birth of his son Emile on August 31.

1876 Second Impressionist exhibition at the Durand-Ruel Gallery. Edouard Duranty published "La Nouvelle Peinture." Gauguin's *Landscape at Viroflay* at the Salon. Started to collect paintings.

1877 First sculptures. Birth of his daughter Aline, his favorite child, on December 24. Third Impressionist exhibition.

1879 Schuffenecker introduced him to Pissarro, who had a great influence on his early work. Showed a sculpture at the Impressionist exhibition. Birth of his son Clovis on May 10.

1880 Moved to a spacious house at 8 Rue Carcel, in the Parisian suburb of Vaugirard, where he had a garden and a large studio. His art collection included works by all the Impressionists, and also by Johan Jongkind, Manet, and Honoré Daumier. Showed one sculpture and seven oils at the Impressionist exhibition. His paintings — *Study of a*

Return from the Hunt, ca 1902
Traced monotype
on off-white laid paper
12⅝" × 16⁷⁄₁₆" (32.2 × 41.8 cm)
Städelsches Kunstinstitut, Francfort

Nude or *Suzanne Sewing* in particular — were favorably reviewed by the critic J.K. Huysmans.

1881   In spite of Monet's and Renoir's protest, Gauguin showed eight oils and two sculptures at the Impressionist exhibition. Birth of his son Jean-René on April 12. Gauguin joined Cézanne, Armand Guillaumin, and Pissarro at Pontoise during the summer. Cézanne deeply influenced Gauguin for several years. However, some misunderstanding created a long-lasting enmity between the two men.

1882   Showed one sculpture and twelve paintings at the Impressionist exhibition, which were harshly criticized by Renoir, Monet, and even Huysmans.

1883   Gauguin and Schuffenecker lost their job at Bertin in January. He regarded this reversal in fortune as an opportunity to dedicate himself to art. Worked with Pissarro at Osny. Birth of his son Pola on December 6.

1884   Spent eight months at Rouen, where Pissarro was working. In the face of growing financial difficulties, he sent his wife and children in November to Copenhagen, to stay near her family. She settled there and started working as a French teacher.

1885   Left for Copenhagen, where he worked as the Scandinavian representative of the company Dillies from Roubaix, makers of tarpaulins. His in-laws showed little understanding for his ambition as an artist and his poor economic circumstances. His one-man show was a failure. In June he returned penniless to Paris, with his son Clovis. Led a life of extreme poverty, working at odd jobs. At the end of September, he left Clovis with his sister and traveled to Dieppe and England.

1886   Took part in the eighth Impressionist exhibition with one sculpture and eighteen oils revealing Pissarro's influence (a still life and landscapes of Rouen, Normandy, and Denmark). Favorable review from the avant-garde critic Félix Fénéon. Sold a painting to the engraver Félix Bracquemond, an old friend of Manet, and this enabled him to spend the summer at Pont-Aven, in Brittany, where he met Émile Bernard in August. This small port had already attracted many landscape painters from America, England, and Scandinavia. Returned to Paris in November, where he met Van Gogh. Bracquemond introduced him to the ceramist Ernest Chaplet. An aborted joint venture in ceramics inspired Gauguin to create a series of ceramic sculptures. In December Gauguin spent twenty-seven days in hospital.

1887   Stay in Paris until April. Clovis was sent back to Denmark. Sailed in April for Panama and later Martinique with the painter Charles Laval. Returned to France in December and stayed with Schuffenecker.

1888   Second stay at Pont-Aven, with Émile Bernard. Met Paul Sérusier. Gauguin came into his own style. Birth of Synthetism, which abandoned the tenets of plein-air painting and emphasized the role of memory and reinterpretation to discover the structure of the object. Theo van Gogh organized his first one-man show at Boussod and Valadon: ceramics and paintings from Martinique and Brittany, which received favorable reviews from the critic Roger Marx. Left for Arles in October, where he stayed for two months with Van Gogh. On December 24, Van Gogh went mad. Gauguin returned to Paris and stayed with Schuffenecker.

1889   Showed seventeen paintings of Martinique, Brittany, and Arles at the exhibition of the Peintres Impressionnistes et Synthétistes organized by Schuffenecker at the Café Volpini. They caused a derisive stir. Took part in the Salon des XX in Brussels. Third stay in Brittany: He returned to Pont-Aven in April, where he spent the summer; in October he settled at Le Pouldu. Executed eleven zincographs. Featured in an exhibition of French and Nordic Impressionists in Copenhagen.

1890   Back in Paris in late January. Stayed with Schuffenecker, at whose house he met Georges Daniel de Monfreid who was to become his closest friend. Returned to Le Pouldu in June. In Paris in December, where he stayed with Schuffenecker.

1891   Became an habitué of the Café Voltaire, where the meetings of the Symbolist writers were held. Octave Mirbeau published an article on Gauguin in February in the "Echo de Paris." In March, Aurier published another one in the "Mercure de France." Sale of thirty paintings on February 23, at the Hotel Drouot, to raise money for his trip to Tahiti. Degas purchased his *Portrait of La Belle Angèle* and a landscape of Martinique. Quick visit to Copenhagen. Took part in the eighth Salon des XX in Brussels. In March, there was a farewell banquet in his honor at the Café Volpini, Mallarmé presiding. Arrived in Tahiti in June, where he settled in the district of Mataiea, south of Papeete, with a native *vahiné*, Tehura.

1893   Returned to France in August. Death of his uncle Isidore, from whom he inherited a share of his estate. Rented a studio on the Rue Vercingétorix, where he lived with Annah the Javanese. First woodcuts. At Degas's urging Durand-Ruel organized a one-man show in November (38 Tahiti paintings, 6 Brittany canvases, and 2 sculptures). Sold eleven paintings. The show made a profound impression on Bonnard, Vuillard, and the Nabis. Took part in the second exhibition of the Peintres Impressionnistes et Symbolistes.

1894   Visit to Bruges to see Memling's paintings. Trip to Copenhagen in January, where he saw his wife and children for the last time. Finished ten woodcuts, a small edition of which was printed by his friend Louis Roy. Took part in the first Salon de la Libre Esthétique in the spring in Brussels. Stayed in Pont-Aven and Le Pouldu from April to December, with Annah. Executed more woodcuts and experimented with watercolor transfer monotypes. In May, broke his leg in a brawl with sailors. Return to Paris, where Annah disappeared after having stolen all the valuables from Gauguin's studio. Worked on *Noa Noa* with Charles Morice.

1895   Attended a banquet in honor of Pierre Puvis de Chavannes. Decided to return to Tahiti. An auction sale of his paintings at the Hotel Drouot failed to raise the money necessary for the trip. Managed to leave nevertheless. Arrived in Tahiti in July and settled in the district of Pounaoouia, on the west coast. He built a large house in the native style.

1896   Worked on *Noa Noa* and *Diverses Choses*. Great solitude and physical suffering.

1897   *Noa Noa* was published in the "Revue Blanche." Death of his daughter Aline, after which Gauguin ceased to write to his wife. Stay in hospital. Works shown at the fourth Salon de la Libre Esthétique in Brussels.

1898   Attempted suicide in January, followed by a period of great productivity. Agreed to do odd jobs. Began a new series of woodcuts. Exhibition in December at Vollard's.

1899   Began writing for "Les Guêpes" in June and started to publish his own satirical journal, "Le Sourire" in August. First traced monotypes.

1900   Death of his son Clovis. Ill most of the year, with no money for medical treatment. Did not paint that year. In hospital at the end of December. Sent ten large monotypes to Vollard. Included in the Centennial Exhibition of French Art 1800-1889 at the World Fair.

1901   In August moved to Atuana, on the island of Hivaoa, in the Marquesas.

1902   Wrote "Avant et Après" in January and February. Sick with eczema and a bad heart. His long-time friend de Monfreid dissuaded him from returning to France.

1903   In April he was sentenced to three months imprisonment for protesting the authorities' treatment of the natives. Gauguin died on May 8. Gauguin exhibitions at the Salon d'Automne and at Vollard's (including 50 paintings).

1906   Daniel de Monfreid organized a Gauguin retrospective at the Salon d'Automne with 227 works.

BIBLIOGRAPHY

CATALOGUES RAISONNÉS

GUÉRIN, Marcel. *L'Œuvre gravé de Gauguin*. 2 vols. Paris: Floury, 1927.

KORNFELD, Eberhard, Joachim HAROLD, and Elizabeth MORGAN. *Paul Gauguin. Catalogue raisonné of his prints*. Bern, 1988.

LEWANDOWSKI, Herbert. *Erste Fassung eines Œuvre Katalogue für Gauguins Gemälde*. Olten: Delphi Verlag, 1950.

WILDENSTEIN, Georges and Raymond COGNIAT. *Gauguin: Catalogue I*. Paris: Les Beaux-Arts, 1964.

WRITINGS BY PAUL GAUGUIN

Ancien culte mahorie. Facsimile edition. With an introduction by René Huyghe, «La Clef de Noa-Noa.» Ed. by Pierre Berès. Paris: La Palme 1951.

Avant et après. Written in the Marquesas Islands in 1903. Facsimile editions, Leipzig: Kurt Wolff Verlag, 1918; Paris: Druet, 1919; Paris: Crès, 1923; Copenhagen: Scripta, 1951. Condensed English edition, *The Intimate Journals*. Tr. by Van Wyck Brooks. Preface by Emil Gauguin. New York: Crown, 1936; Bloomington, Indiana: Indiana University Press - Midland Books, 1956.

Cahier pour Aline. Facsimile edition. Ed. and notes by Suzanne Damion. Paris: n.p., 1963.

Correspondance de Paul Gauguin. Documents, témoignages. Ed. by Victor Merlhes. Paris: Fondation Singer-Polignac, 1984.

Letters to Ambroise Vollard and André Fontainas. Ed. by John Rewald. Tr. by G. Mack. San Francisco: The Grabhorn Press, 1943.

Lettres de Gauguin à André Fontainas. Paris: Librairie de France, 1921.

Lettres de Gauguin à Daniel de Monfreid. With a tribute by Victor Segalen. Paris: Crès, 1919; Plon, 1930. New ed. by Annie Joly-Segalen, Paris: Georges Falaize, 1950. *Letters to Daniel de Monfreid*. Tr. by Ruth Pielkovo, with a foreword by Frederick O'Brien. New York: Dodd, Mead & Co., 1922.

Lettres de Gauguin à Emile Bernard. Tonnerre, France: Edition de la Rénovation esthétique, 1926. Brussels: Nouvelle Revue, 1942. Ed. by M.A. Bernard-Fort. Geneva: P. Cailler, 1954.

Lettres de Gauguin à sa femme et à ses amis. Ed. by Maurice Malingue. Paris: Grasset, 1946, 1949. *Letters to His Wife and Friends*. Tr. by H. Stenning, Cleveland, 1949.

45 Lettres à Vincent, Théo et Jo van Gogh, Collection Rijksmuseum Vincent van Gogh, Amsterdam. Ed. by Douglas Cooper. The Hague: Straatsuitgeverij, 1893.

Noa Noa. Paris: La Plume, 1900; Crès, 1924. Facsimile edition, Berlin: Marees, 1926. Tr. by O.F. Theis. New York: Lear, 1947; The Noonday Press, 1957. New ed., *Noa Noa, Gauguin's Tahiti*. Ed. by Nicholas Wadley. Tr. by Jonathan Griffin. Oxford: Phaidon, 1985.

Oviri - Ecrits d'un sauvage. Ed. and notes by Pierre Dorival. Paris: Gallimard, 1974. *The Writings of a Savage: Paul Gauguin*. Ed. by Daniel Guérin, with an introdution by Wayne Andersen. Tr. by Eleanor Levieux. New York: Viking, 1978.

Racontars de rapin. Paris: Falaize, 1951.

Le Sourire. satirical journal, written, illustrated, and duplicated by Paul Gauguin. Facsimile edition. Introduction and notes by L.-J. Bugue. Paris: G.-P. Maisonneuve et Cie et Max Besson Libraire, 1952.

BOOKS ON GAUGUIN

ALEXANDRE, Arsène. *Paul Gauguin, sa vie et le sens de son œuvre*. Paris: Bernheim-Jeune, 1930.

AMISHAI-MAISELS, Ziva. *Gauguin's religious themes*. New York: Garland, 1985. Based on the author's doctoral thesis, Hebrew University, 1969.

ANDERSEN, Wayne. *Gauguin's Paradise Lost*. New York: Viking, 1971.

BARTH, Wilhelm. *Paul Gauguin 1848-1903*. Catalogue of the exhibition at the Kunsthalle. Basel, 1928.

BARTH, Wilhelm. *Paul Gauguin. Das Leben, der Mensch und der Künstler*. Basel 1929.

BECKER, Beril. *Paul Gauguin. The Calm Madman*. New York: Tudor, 1935.

BERNARD, Emile. *Souvenirs inédits sur l'artiste peintre Paul Gauguin et ses compagnons*. Lorient, France: Imprimerie du Nouvelliste du Morbihan.

BODELSEN, Merete Christensen. *Gauguin's Ceramics: A Study in the Development of His Art*. London: Faber & Faber Ltd, 1964.

BODELSON, Merete Christensen. *Gauguin og Impressionisterne*. Copenhagen: Kunstforeningen, 1968.

BURNETT, Robert. *The Life of Paul Gauguin*. London: Cobden-Sanderson, 1936; New York: Oxford University Press, 1937.

CACHIN, Françoise. *Gauguin*. Paris: Le Livre de Poche, 1967.

CHASSÉ, Charles. *Gauguin et le groupe de Pont-Aven*. Paris: Floury, 1921.

CHASSÉ, Charles. *Gauguin et son temps*. Paris: Bibliothèque des Arts, 1955.

CHASSÉ, Charles. *Gauguin sans légendes*. Paris, 1965.

COGNIAT, Raymond. *Gauguin, ses amis, l'école de Pont-Aven et l'Académie Julian*. Catalogue of the exhibition at the Galerie des Beaux-Arts. Introduction by Maurice Denis. Paris, 1934.

COGNIAT, Raymond. *La Vie ardente de Paul Gauguin*. Exhibition catalogue. Introduction by Henri Focillon. Paris: Editions Gazette des Beaux-Arts, 1936.

COGNIAT, Raymond. *Paul Gauguin*. Paris: Braun, 1938.

COGNIAT, RAYMOND. *Gauguin*. Paris: Tisné, 1947.

COGNIAT, Raymond. *Paul Gauguin: A Sketchbook (1884-1888)*. With a foreword by John Rewald. Reproduced from the original sketchbook owned by Hammer Galleries. Vol. 1 : English ed.; vol. 2: French ed. New York: Hammer Galleries, 1962.

COOPER, Douglas. *Paul Gauguin, Paintings, Sculptures, and Engravings*. Catalogue of the exhibition at the Royal Scottish Academy, Edinburgh, 1955.

DANIELSSON, Bengt. *Gauguins söderhavsär*. Stockholm: Forum, 1964. *Gauguin in the South Seas*. Tr. by Reginald Spink. New York: Doubleday, 1965; London: George Allen & Unwin, 1965.

DANIELSSON, Bengt and Patrick O'REILY. *Gauguin journaliste à Tahiti et ses articles des "Guêpes."* Paris: Société des Océanistes, 1966.

DEL POMAR, F. Cossio and G.D. DE MONFREID. *Gauguin, exposition rétrospective*. Introduction to the exhibition catalogue. Paris, 1926.

DEL POMAR, F. Cossio. *Arte y vida de Pablo Gauguin*. Paris, Madrid: Leon Sanchez Cuesta, 1930.

DENIS, Maurice. *Théories (1890-1910). Du Symbolisme et de Gauguin vers un nouvel ordre classique*. Paris: Bibliothèque de l'Occident, 1912. 4th ed., Paris : L. Rouart & J. Watelin, 1920.

DIETRICH, Linnea Stonesifer. *A Study of Symbolism in the Tahitian painting of Paul Gauguin, 1891-1893*. Unpublished doctoral thesis, University of Delaware, 1973.

DORIVAL, Bernard. *Carnet de Tahiti*. Facsimile edition of a sketchbook from Gauguin's first trip to Tahiti (1891-1893). Paris: Quatre Chemins, 1954.

DORRA, Henri. *Paul Gauguin: His Place in the Meeting of East and West*. Catalogue of the exhibition at the Museum of Fine Arts. Houston, 1954.

DORSENNE, Jean. *La Vie sentimentale de Paul Gauguin*. Paris: Cahiers de la Quinzaine, 1927.

ESTIENNE, Charles. *Gauguin*. Geneva: Skira, 1953. *Gauguin. Biographical and Critical Studies*. Tr. by James Emmons. Geneva: Skira, 1953.

FIELD, Richard S. *Paul Gauguin: The Paintings of the First Voyage to Tahiti.* New York: Garland, 1977. Originally presented as the author's thesis, Harvard, University, 1963.

FLETCHER, John G. *Paul Gauguin, His Life and Work.* New York: Little Brown, 1921.

GAUGUIN, Pola. *My Father, Paul Gauguin.* Tr. from the Norwegian by Arthur G. Chater. London: Cassell, 1937; New York : A.A. Knopf, 1937.

GOLDWATER, Robert J. *Gauguin.* London: Thames & Hudson; New York: Abrams, 1957.

GRABER, Hans. *Paul Gauguin nach eigenen und fremden Zeugnissen.* Basel: B. Schwabe, 1946.

GRAY, Christopher. *Sculpture and Ceramics of Paul Gauguin.* Baltimore, Maryland: The Johns Hopkins Press, 1963.

HALE, Charlotte. *A Study of Paul Gauguin's Correspondence Relating to His Painting Materials and Techniques.* Courtauld Institute Diploma Project, London, 1983.

HANSON, Elizabeth and Lawrence HANSON. *Noble Savage. The Life of Paul Gauguin.* New York: Ramdom House, 1954.

HANSON, Elizabeth and Lawrence HANSON. *The Seekers: Gauguin, Van Gogh, Cézanne.* New York: Ramdom House, 1963.

HARTRICK, A.S. *Paul Gauguin.* Catalogue of the exhibition at the Leicester Galleries. London, 1924.

HAUTECOUR, L. *Gauguin.* Geneva: Skira, 1942.

HOOG, Michel. *Gauguin, vie et œuvre.* Paris: Nathan, 1987.

HUYGHE, René. *Le Carnet de Paul G.* Facsimile edition of a sketchbook from Brittany and Arles. Ed. by René Huyghe. 2 vols. Paris: Quatre Chemins, 1952.

HUYGHE, René ed. *Gauguin.* Paris: Hachette, 1961.

INBODEN, Gudrun. *Mallarmé und Gauguin. Absolute Kunst als Utopie.* Suttgart: J.B. Metzler, 1978.

JAWORSKA, Wladyslava. *Paul Gauguin et l'Ecole de Pont-Aven.* Tr. from the Polish by Simon Laks. Paris: Ides et Calandes, 1971. *Gauguin and the Pont-Aven School.* Tr. by Patrick Evans. Greenwich, Connecticut: New York Graphic Society, 1972.

JIRAT-WASIUTYNSKI, Vojtech. *Paul Gauguin in the Context of Symbolism.* New York: Garland, 1978. Originally presented as the author's thesis, Princeton University, 1975.

KLAUS, Jürgen. *Paul Gauguin.* Catalogue of the exhibition at the Haus der Kunst, Munich. Essay by Germain Bazin. Note by Harold Joachim. 1960.

KUNSTLER, Charles. *Gauguin, peintre maudit.* Paris: Floury, 1934, 1942, 1947.

LE PAUL, Charles-Guy. *L'Impressionnisme dans l'Ecole de Pont-Aven: Monet, Renoir, Gauguin et leurs disciples.* Lausanne, Paris: La Bibliothèque des Arts, 1983.

LEPROHON, P. *Paul Gauguin.* Paris, 1975.

LEYMARIE, Jean. *Gauguin: Exposition du centenaire.* Catalogue of the exhibition at the Orangerie. Introduction by René Huyghe. Paris, 1949.

LEYMARIE, Jean. *Paul Gauguin, Aquarelles, pastels et dessins de couleur.* Basel: Phoebus, 1960. *Paul Gauguin: Watercolours, Pastels and Drawings in Colour.* London: Faber and Faber Ltd, 1961.

LOIZE, Jean. *Les Amitiés du peintre Georges-Daniel de Monfreid et ses reliques de Gauguin.* Paris: Jean Loize, 1951.

LOIZE, Jean. *Noa Noa par Paul Gauguin.* Paris: André Balland, 1966.

McCANN MORLEY, G.L. *Paul Gauguin.* Introduction to the catalogue of the exhibition of paintings and prints by Gauguin at the San Francisco Museum of Art, 1936.

MALINGUE, Maurice. *Gauguin.* Monaco: Documents d'art, 1943.

MALINGUE, Maurice. *Gauguin, le peintre et son œuvre.* 2 vols. Paris: Presse de la Cité, 1948.

MALINGUE, Maurice. *Gauguin et ses amis.* Catalogue of the exhibition at the Galerie Kléber. Paris, 1949.

MARKS-VAN DEN BRONCKE, Ursula Frances. *Gauguin, ses origines et sa formation artistique.* Unpublished doctoral thesis, Sorbonne, Paris.

MARTIN-MÉRY, G. *Gauguin et le groupe de Pont-Aven.* Catalogue of the exhibition at the Musée des Beaux-Arts. Quimper, France, 1950.

MASSON, C. and R. REY. *Sculptures de Gauguin.* Catalogue of the exhibition at the Musée du Luxembourg. Paris, 1927.

MITTELSTÄDT, Kuno. *Die Selbstbildnisse Paul Gauguins.* East-Berlin: Henschelverlag, 1966. Trad. by E.G. Hull, *The Self-Portraits of Paul Gauguin.* Oxford: B. Cassirer, 1968.

MONFREID, Georges Daniel de. *Gauguin.* Introduction to the catalogue of a retrospective exhibition. Paris: Galerie Dru, 1923.

MORICE, Charles. *Œuvres récentes de Paul Gauguin.* Catalogue of the exhibition at the Galerie Durand-Ruel. Paris, 1893.

MORICE, Charles. *Gauguin. Rétrospective.* Introduction to the catalogue of the exhibition at the Salon d'Automne. Paris, 1906.

MORICE, Charles. *Paul Gauguin.* Paris: Floury, 1919.

O'REILLY, Patrick. *Catalogue du Musée Gauguin, Papeari, Tahiti.* Paris: Fondation Singer-Polignac, 1966.

PERRUCHOT, Henri. *Gauguin, sa vie ardente et misérable.* Paris: Le Sillage, 1948.

PERRUCHOT, Henri. *La Vie de Gauguin.* Paris: Hachette, 1961.

PICKVANCE, Ronald. *Gauguin Drawings.* London: Hamlyn, 1969.

PLATTE, Hans. *Paul Gauguin. Ta Matete, der Markt.* Stuttgart: Reclam, 1959.

POPE, Karen Kristine Rechnitzer. *Gauguin and Martinique.* Unpublished doctoral thesis, University of Texas at Austin, 1981.

PUIG, R. *Gauguin, Monfreid et leurs amis.* Perpignan: La Tramontane, 1958.

REWALD, John. *Gauguin.* Paris, London, New York: Hyperion, 1938.

REWALD, John. *Gauguin Drawings.* New York: Yseloff, 1958.

REWALD, John. *Post-Impressionism from Van Gogh to Gauguin.* New York: Museum of Modern Art, 3rd ed., 1978.

REY, Robert. *Gauguin.* Paris: Rieder, 1923, 1928, 1939. Tr. by F.C. de Sumichrast. London, 1924.

REY, Robert. *Onze menus de Paul Gauguin, Menus propos de Robert Rey.* Geneva: Cramer, 1950.

ROOKMAAKER, Hendrik Roelof. *Gauguin and 19th Century Art Theory.* Amsterdam: Swets & Zeitlinger, 1972. Revision of the author's doctoral thesis published in 1959.

ROSKILL, M.W. *Van Gogh, Gauguin and the Impressionist Circle.* Greenwich, Connecticut: New York Graphic Society, 1970.

ROSTRUP, H. *Paul Gauguin.* Catalogue of the exhibition at the Ny Carlsberg Glyptotek. Copenhagen, 1948.

ROTONCHAMP, Jean de. *Paul Gauguin.* Weimar: Kessler, 1906. Paris: Druet, 1906; Crès, 1925.

SEGALEN, Victor. *Gauguin dans son dernier décor, et autres textes de Tahiti.* Montpellier, France: Fata Morgana, 1974.

SCHMIDT, Georg. *Paul Gauguin.* Catalogue of the exhibition at the Kunstmuseum. Basel, 1949-1950.

STERNHEIM, Carl. *Gauguin und Van Gogh.* Berlin: Die Schmiede, 1924.

SYKOROVA, Libuse. *Gauguin Woodcuts.* London: Hamlyn, 1963.

TEILHET-FISK, Jehanne. *Paradise Reviewed: An Interpretation of Gauguin's Polynesian Symbolism.* Revision of the author's doctoral thesis, University of California at Los Angeles, 1975. Ann Arbor, Michigan: University of Michigan Press, 1983.

TOW, Martin. *Tainted Paradise. A Study of the Life and Art of Paul Gauguin.* Camden, New Jersey: Haddon Craftsmen, 1937.

VANCE, Mary Lynn Zink. *Gauguin's Polynesian Pantheon as a Visual Language.* Ann Arbor, Michigan: University Microfilms International. Based on the author's doctoral thesis, Univeristy of California at Santa Barbara, 1983.

VAN DOWSKI, L. *Paul Gauguin. Das abenteuerliche Leben des grossen Malers.* Bern, 1948.

VIIRLAID, H.K. *The Concept of Vision in Paul Gauguin's "Vision après le sermon."* Doctoral thesis. Ottawa: National Library of Canada, 1980.

WAGSTAFF, Samuel J. and Claus VIRCH. *Gauguin: Paintings, Drawings, Prints, Sculptures.* Catalogue of the exhibition at the Art Institute, Chicago, and the Metropolitan Museum of Art, New York. Introduction by Théodore Rousseau. 1959.

WIESE, E. *Paul Gauguin. Zwei Jahrzehnte nach seinem Tode.* Leipzig, 1923.

WILDENSTEIN, Daniel. *Paul Gauguin.* Milan: Fratelli Fabbri, 1972.

EXHIBITIONS

1966 *Gauguin and the Pont-Aven Group.* Introduction by Denys Sutton. Catalogue de Ronald Pickvance. Arts Council, The Tate Gallery, Londres.
Gauguin and the Decorative Style. Introduction by Lawrence Alloway. Essays by Marilyn Hunt and Rose-Carol Wasthon. The Solomon Guggenheim Museum, New York.
Gauguin und sein Kreis in der Bretagne. Kunsthaus, Zurich.

1968 *Neo-Impressionism.* Catalogue by Robert L. Herbert. The Solomon Guggenheim Museum, New York.

1969 *Gauguin and Exotic Art.* Essays by Bengt Danielsson, William H. Davenport, and Richard S. Field. University Museum, University of Pennsylvania, Philadelphia.
Gauguin. National musée of Modern Art, Tokyo; National Museum of Modern Art, Kyoto.

1971 *Le Temps de Gauguin.* Musée municipal, Brest, France.
The Early Work of Paul Gauguin, Genesis of an Artist. Introduction by Richard J. Boyle. Cincinnati Art Museum.
Prints by Paul Gauguin. Introduction by Colter Feller Ives. Metropolitan Museum of Art, New York.

1973 *Paul Gauguin: Monotypes.* Catalogue by Richard Field. Philadelphia Museum of Art.

1977 *Le Post-Impressionnisme.* Palais de Tokyo, Paris.

1978 *Paul Gauguin. Das Druckgraphische Werk.* Catalogue by A. Haase et al. Museum Villa Stuck, Munich.
L'Ecole de Pont-Aven dans les collections publiques and privées de Bretagne. Museums of Quimper, Rennes and Nantes, France.
Paul Gauguin. Essay by Pierre Leprohon. Salon d'Automne, Paris.

1979 *Post-Impressionism: Cross Currents in European Painting.* Catalogue by John House. London: Royal Academy of Arts.
Gauguin à la Martinique: le musée imaginaire complet de ses peintures, dessins, sculptures and céramiques, les faux, les lettres, les catalogues d'exposition. Catalogue by Roger Cucchi. Calivran Anstalt, Vaduz, Liechtenstein.

1981 *Gauguin et les chefs-d'œuvre de l'Ordrupgaard de Copenhague.* Introduction by Yves Brayer. Musée Marmottan, Paris.

1982 *Gauguin to Moore. Primitivism in Modern Sculpture.* Art Gallery of Ontario, Toronto.

1984 *Gauguin and Van Gogh in Copenhagen in 1893.* Catalogue by Merete Christensen Bodelsen. Ordrupgaard, Copenhagen.

1985 *Le Chemin de Gauguin. Genèse et rayonnement.* Musée départmental du Prieuré, Saint-Germain-en-Laye, Yvelines, France.

1986 *Cent ans: Gauguin à Pont-Aven.* Musée de Pont-Aven.

1988-1989 *The Art of Paul Gauguin.* Catalogue by Richard Brettell et al. National Gallery of Art, Washington, D.C.; The Art Institute of Chicago; Galeries Nationales du Grand Palais, Paris.

We wish to thank the owners of the pictures reproduced herein, as well as those collectors who did not want to have their name mentioned. Our special thanks to the Galerie Schmit in Paris and Acquavella Galleries and E.V. Thaw & Co. in New York for their help.

BELGIUM: Musées Royaux des Beaux-Arts de Belgique, *Brussels.*

DENMARK: Ny Carlsberg Glyptotek, *Copenhagen* - Ordrupgaardsamlingen, *Charlottenlund-Copenhagen.*

FEDERAL REPUBLIC OF GERMANY: Museum Folkwang, *Essen* - Städelsches Kunstinstitut, *Francfort* - Kunsthalle, *Hamburg* - Bayerische Staatsgemäldesammlungen, Neue Pinakothek, *Munich.*

FRANCE: Musée des Beaux-Arts, *Grenoble* - Bibliothèque nationale, *Paris* - Collection Manoukian, *Paris* - Musée d'Orsay, *Paris* - Musées des Arts décoratifs, *Paris* - Musée des Arts océaniens et africains, *Paris* - Musée du Louvre, *Paris* - Musée Marmottan, *Paris* - Musée de *Rouen.*

NETHERLANDS: Rijksmuseum Vincent van Gogh, *Amsterdam.*

NORWAY: Nasjonalgalleriet, *Oslo.*

SWITZERLAND: Kupferstichkabinett der öffentlichen Kunstsammlung, *Basel* - Rudolf Staechelin, *Basel.*

UNITED KINGDOM: National Gallery, *Edinburgh* - Courtauld Institute Galleries, *London.*

U.S.A.: Museum of Art, *Baltimore* - Museum of Fine Arts, *Boston* - The Albright-Knox Art Gallery, *Buffalo, N. Y.* - The Fogg Art Museum, *Cambridge, Mass.* - The Art Institute, *Chicago* - The *Cleveland* Museum of Art - Wadsworth Atheneum, *Hartford, Conn.* - The Nelson-Atkins Museum of Art, *Kansas City, Missouri* - The Armand Hammer Foundation, *Los Angeles* - Artemis Group, *New York* - The Metropolitan Museum of Art, *New York* - Mr. and Mrs. Eugene V. Thaw, *New York* - The Chrysler Museum of Art, *Norfolk, Va.* - Smith College Museum of Art, *Northampton, Mass.* - The *Philadelphia* Museum of Art - The Fine Arts Museums of *San Francisco* - The *Toledo* Museum of Art - The National Gallery of Art, *Washington, D.C.*

PHOTOGRAPHS

Hinz, Allschwill-Basel - Ole Woldbye, Copenhagen - Ursula Edelmann, Francfort - Jacques Betant, Lausanne - Otto E. Nelson, New York - Jacques Lathion, Oslo - Service Photographique de la Réunion des Musées Nationaux, Paris - Studio Lourmel, Photo Routhier, Paris - Artothek, Planegg/Munich.

ILLUSTRATIONS

Above the Abyss 23
Adam and Eve 90
Arlésienne: Madame Ginoux (L') 28
Auti te pape 62
Awakening of Spring 49

Barbaric Tales 81
Belle Angèle (La) 41
Blond Harvest (The) 27
Blue Trees 22
Bouquet of Flowers 87
Breton Boy 36
Breton Boys Bathing 32
Breton Landscape 26
Breton Woman Seen from the Back 33
Breton Women 40
Breton Women in Front of a Fence 38
By the Pond 19

Calvary (The) 35
Cellist (The) 43
Crouching Marquesan Woman 84
Crouching Tahitian Girl 56

Delicious Earth 60
Dream (The) 75
Dreamer (The) 59

Emile Gauguin 9

Faaturuma 59
Flight 88, 90
Ford (The) 88
Four Breton Girls Dancing 30

Garden in Winter, Rue Carcel (The) 12
Girl with a Fan 83
Grape Gathering at Arles 70
Grasshoppers and the Ants (The) 25
Green Christ (The) 35

Head of a Tahitian 77
Head of a Tahitian Woman 61, 77
Head of a Young Man 53
Head of Peasant Girl 37
Human Misery 70

Jacob Wrestling with the Angel 31

Landscape at Pont-Aven 13
Little Breton Boy 16
Little Breton Boy Carrying a Jug 14
Loss of Virginity (Study for The) 48
Loss of Virginity (The) 49

Madame Mette Gauguin 10
Manao Tupapau 54, 68, 69
Maori Woman with Hat 51
Market Gardens at Vaugirard (The) 5
Martinique Landscape 17
Maruru 67

Nafea Faa Ipoipo 57
Nativity 72
Nave Nave Fenua 60

Nevermore 76
Nirvana 47
No Te Aha Oe Riri? 74
Noa Noa 63

Parahi Te Marae 66
Parau Na Te Varaua Ino 65
Pastoral Scene, Martinique 24
Paul Gauguin and Camille Pissarro 6
Picking Mangoes 18
Poèmes Barbares 73
Pont-Aven, The Village 71
Portrait of a Young Girl 44
Portrait of Madeleine Bernard 29
Portrait of Meyer De Haan 47
Portrait of Stéphane Mallarmé 39
Portrait of Upaupa Schneklud 43
Profile of Boy 8

Return from the Hunt 91
Riders on the Beach 89
Roman Burial Ground at Arles (The) 20

Schuffenecker Family (The) 42
Seated Breton Girl 15
Seated Maori Figure 50
Self-Portrait 7
Self-Portraits 6
She Thinks of the Specter 54
Sleeping Boy 9
Specter Watches over Her (The) 68, 69
Street in Tahiti 52
Study of a Nude 11
Suzanne Sewing 11

Tahitian Couple Walking 90
Tahitian on Horseback 88
Tahitian Woman with Evil Spirit 80, 85
Te Rerioa 75
Thank You 67
There Is the Temple 66
Title page of the journal Le Sourire 55
Two Breton Women 21
Two Tahitian Women 82

Vahine No Te Vi 58
Vaïté Goupil 44
Vision of the Sermon 31

When Will You Marry? 57
Where Do We Come From? 78-79
Where Do We Come From? (Study for) 78
White Horse (The) 86
Why Are You Angry? 74
Willow (The) 26
Woman in the Waves 46
Woman with Mango 58
Women at the River 62
Words of the Devil 65
Words of the Devil (Eve) 64

Yellow Christ (The) 34
Yellow Haystacks (The) 27
Young Girl (detail) 45